THE DOUG SKINNER SONGBOOK

THE DOUG SKINNER SONGBOOK

WORDS AND MUSIC BY DOUG SKINNER

BLACK SCAT BOOKS
2017

THE DOUG SKINNER SONGBOOK
Words & Music by Doug Skinner

ISBN 13 978-0-9992622-2-1

For additional information contact the publisher:
blackscatbooks@icloud.com

ACKNOWLEDGMENTS:
"Peepee Caca Fucky-Fuck" appeared in *Oulipo Pornobongo: Anthology of Erotic Wordplay* (Black Scat Books: 2016)

Cover art by the author

BLACK SCAT BOOKS
Sublime Art & Literature
BlackScatBooks.net

CONTENTS

Introduction ... 9
Bandwagon ... 11
Bloated Plutocrats on Parade ... 14
Breeders Can't Be Choosers ... 17
Buenas Noches, Little Roaches ... 20
Careers ... 22
The Death of Orpheus ... 23
A Different Point of View ... 24
Don't Despair ... 26
Don't Talk to Me ... 28
Fa La La La La ... 30
A Few Essential Principles ... 32
Film Crew ... 34
Flake Food ... 36
Get on the Grid ... 38
Good Night ... 40
The Hypnotist's Birthday ... 43
I Just Don't Understand ... 46
If Something Goes Wrong, Just Pretend It Didn't Happen ... 48
In Memoriam ... 49
It's Easy to Be an Eccentric Nowadays ... 52
James ... 54
Let the Patient Lift the Panniculus ... 56
Let's Ridicule the Nightingale ... 58
Little Flower ... 60
Little Two-Headed Kitten ... 62
Love Me Unconditionally ... 64
Make a Wish ... 66
Medulla Oblongata ... 68
My Face Is in the Sand ... 70
My Pal Satan ... 72
Notary Publics ... 75
Oh Dear, Oh Dear (Maman, Maman) ... 78
Peepee Caca Fucky-Fuck ... 79
People Like You ... 80
Ptooey ... 82
The Renaissance Faire ... 84
The Rose ... 87
Somebody Said Something Offensive ... 88
Son of a Gun ... 90
Uncle's Ankles ... 92
Viola ...94
We All Work So Hard ... 98
We Need More Art ... 101
The Worse It Gets, the Better We Like It ... 104
Worthless Little Moments ... 108
Your Parents ... 111

INTRODUCTION

The songs in this collection were performed in a variety of clubs, cabarets, and theaters, mostly in NYC. I accompanied myself on ukulele or piano, often with other musicians, particularly Carol Benner or David Gold on viola, Doug Roesch on guitar, and Ralph Hamperian on tuba. Some were written for the trio White Knuckle Sandwich, in which I was joined by Jennifer Perez and Anne Shapiro.

Some were recorded for the albums *That Regrettable Weekend* (at this writing, available on Bandcamp) and *White Knuckle Sandwich* (released years ago on a quaint device called a "CD").

The songs are, I hope, suitable for many occasions. They enliven parties, stimulate sales in bars, provoke discussion in the classroom, earn quarters on the subway. You can play them anywhere. Chord symbols above the staff permit you, or an obliging colleague, to provide a harmonic underpinning on any instrument that plays several notes at once. I suppose you could also play the tunes on a melody instrument, like a clarinet, and just think the lyrics to yourself. I never tried that. None is particularly erotic, so you don't have to worry about unwanted advances; none is suitable for dancing or singalongs, to your eternal gratitude. Many use more than three chords and one time signature, which helps teach arithmetic. Our workforce cannot remain competitive without a solid grounding in the sciences.

I hope you enjoy them. Rev up those vocal cords!

Doug Skinner
New Paltz, NY
August 2017

BANDWAGON

LIVELY
C Dm7 C G7 C Dm7 C G7
mf
mf
THERE'S A
C Dm7 C G7 C Dm7
BAND- WAGON HEADED DOWN THE MIDDLE OF THE STREET. BETTER GET YOURSELF A TICKET, BETTER
C G7 F Fm
GET YOURSELF A SEAT, OR YOU WILL FIND YOU'VE BEEN LEFT BE- HIND AND IG-
C G(B bass) B♭dim7 D7 G7
NORED. THERE'S A BAND- WAGON COMING, YOU BETTER JUMP ON BOARD!
C Cdim7 Dm7 G7 C Cdim7 Dm7 G7
ALL A- BOARD! WELL, IT'S
C Dm C G7 C Dm7
GETTING KIND OF CROWDED BUT THERE'S STILL A LOT OF ROOM. IT- 'LL KEEP YOU SAFE AND COZY AND PRO-
C G7 F Fm
TECT YOU FROM THE GLOOM. SO DROP YOUR PRIDE AND JUST HITCH A RIDE WITH THE
C G(B bass) B♭dim7 D7 G7
HORDE. THERE'S A BAND- WAGON COMING, YOU BETTER JUMP ON BOARD!

C Cdim7 Dm7 G7 C Cdim7 Dm7 G7
ALL A- BOARD! 'CAUSE
Bm7 E7 Am7 D7
IF YOU FUSS AND QUES- TION, YOU'LL RU- IN YOUR DI- GES- TION. SO
Dm7 G7 Dm7 G7 C C♯dim7 Dm7 G7
JUST RE-LAX, DON'T O- VER-TAX YOUR POOR BELEAGUERED BRAIN. IT
Bm7 E7 Am7 D7
DOES-N'T PAY TO TRUN- DLE THAT SOL- I- TAR- Y BUN- DLE, SO
Dm7 G7 Dm7 G7 Dm7 G7
DROP YOUR PACK, AND JUST SIT BACK, AND SAVE YOURSELF THE STRAIN. THERE'S A
C Dm7 C G7 C Dm7
BAND- WAGON HEADED DOWN THE MIDDLE OF THE STREET. IF YOU GET YOURSELF A TICKET, YOU CAN
C G7 F Fm
PUT UP YOUR FEET. DON'T TREAD THE PATH WHERE THE GRAPES OF WRATH ARE
C G (B bass) B♭dim7 D7 G7
STORED. THERE'S A BAND- WAGON COMING, YOU BETTER JUMP ON BOARD!

C
Cdim7
Dm7
C
Cdim7
Dm7
G7
ALL A- BOARD!
ALL A-
C
Cdim7
Dm7
G7
C
Cdim7
Dm7
G7
BOARD!
ALL A- BOARD!
f
THERE'S A
D7
G7
C
Cdim7
Dm7
G7
C
BANDWAGON COMING,
YOU BETTER GET ON BOARD!

FEBRUARY 1995
N.Y.C.

Bloated Plutocrats on Parade

MARTIAL
B♭ B♭ B♭ B♭
mf mf
BLOATED PLUTOCRATS ON PA- RADE. THEY'RE THE
E♭ D7 Gm E♭ D7
MUL-TI-MILLIONAIRES WHO MAKE THE GRADE. THEY'RE AS RICH AS KINGS AND QUEENS, LOUNGING
Gm E♭7 C7 F7 B♭ F7
IN THEIR LIMOUSINES, WAVING AT THE PEO-PLE WITH THE MONEY THAT THEY MADE. BLOATED
B♭ B♭ E♭ D7
PLUTOCRATS ON PA- RADE. THEY'RE RE- LAX-ING IN THEIR STATELY MOTOR-
Gm E♭ D7 Gm E♭7
CADE. THEY'RE AS RICH AS QUEENS AND KINGS, THEY HAVE LOTS OF PRETTY THINGS.
C7 F7 B♭ F7 B♭ A♭
THEY'RE OUR LORDS AND MASTERS AND THEY'RE MEANT TO BE OBEYED. THEY'RE RICH, THEY'RE
E♭ Fm B♭7 E♭ D7
RICH. THEY RULE THE HU- MAN RACE. THEY ITCH, THEY
Gm Cm D7 Gm F7
ITCH TO KEEP US IN OUR PLACE. SOME OTH-ER SYSTEM MIGHT BE

B♭ C7 F7 B♭
MORE FAIR. BUT THEY TELL US THAT WOULD BE CLASS WARFARE. BLOATED PLUTOCRATS ON PA-
B♭ E♭ D7 Gm
RADE. LOOK AT ALL THAT POMP AND PRIVI- LEGE DIS- PLAYED. IT'S A-
E♭ D7 Gm E♭7 C7 F7
MAZING WHAT THEY EARN, THEY HAVE CASH ENOUGH TO BURN. ONE COULD EVEN SAY THEY'RE OVER-
B♭ Gm Gm Gm
mp
PAID. MONEY'S SUCH A FUN-NY THING THAT
Cm Gm D7
I CAN'T HELP FROM WONDERING IF MAY- BE THEY SHOULD DO AWHILE WITH - OUT IT.
D7 Gm Cm
PICTURE ALL THE PLU-TO-CRATS IN SHABBY PANTS AND PAPER HATS COM-
Gm F7 Gm
PELLED TO SLEEP ON RAGS AND MATS AND FORCED TO FIGHT FOR FOOD WITH RATS, COULD YOU SUPPRESS A SMILE? I
D7 F7 B♭ B♭
mf
DOUBT IT. BLOATED PLUTOCRATS ON PA- RADE. AND THEIR

E♭ D7 Gm E♭ D7
POW-ER O- VER US WILL NEV-ER FADE. THEY GET CAVALCADES OF CASH WHILE WE
Gm E♭7 C7 F7 B♭
FUMBLE IN THE TRASH, AND THEY LOOK DOWN SERENE AND UN-A- FRAID.
C7 F7 B♭
THEY LOOK DOWN SERENE AND UN-A- FRAID.

FEBRUARY 2017
NEW PALTZ, N.Y.

BREEDERS CAN'T BE CHOOSERS

FREELY
Am E7 Am E7
f
Am Dm E7 Dm
mp
YES, WHEN YOU WERE YOUNGER, YOU GOT A LIT- TLE WILD. YOU COP- U-LATED WITH YOUR MATE AND
B7 E7 G7 C
GAVE THE WORLD A CHILD, A CHILD YOU HOPED TO CONTEMPLATE WITH PLEASURE AND WITH PRIDE.
E7 Am G7
THOSE HOPES HAVE DIED. BUT AS YOU TURN A-WAY IN SHAME AND
C Dm B7 E7
HIDE YOUR WEEPING FACE, RE- MEMBER THAT OLD AX- I- OM THAT GUIDES THE HUMAN RACE. SO IF YOUR
FAIRLY FAST
Am Am D7 D7
mf
HEART IS FILLED WITH GRIP- ING WHEN YOUR KID WON'T DO HIS WIP- ING, JUST RE-
TAKES IN TO HIS TEACH-ER SOME DE- CAY- ING ROADKILL CREATURE, JUST RE-
(INSTRUMENTAL)
B7 B7 E7 E7
MEM- BER, BREEDERS CAN'T BE CHOOSERS. AND WHEN HE
MEM- BER, BREEDERS CAN'T BE CHOOSERS. AND WHEN HIS

Am
Am
D7
D7
TAKES HIS LIT- TLE PIS- TOL AND PLAYS COW- BOY WITH YOUR CRYS- TAL, JUST RE-
WAY TO COPE WITH SHYNESS IS STICK- ING FIN- GERS UP HIS SINUS- ES, JUST RE-
G7
G7
E7
E7
MEM- BER, BREEDERS CAN'T BE CHOOSERS. YOU
MEM- BER, BREEDERS CAN'T BE CHOOSERS. YOU
YEA,
C#7
C#7
F#m
F#m
CRAVED A CHILD WHO CAR- RIED YOUR OWN D. N. A., AND NOW HE'S
CRAVED A CHILD WHO BORE YOUR OWN GE- NET- IC CODE, AND SO YOU
FROM THY MIGHT- Y LOINS THOU HAST PRO- DUCED A SON, AND HE'S AN
D7
D7
B7
B7
HERE TO STAY, AND HE'S A LOATHSOME BRAT. RAT A TAT A TAT.
SPAWNED A TOAD WHO LOOKS A LOT LIKE YOU. COCKADOODLEDOO.
UG- LY ONE, FOR HE RE- SEM- BLES THEE. GOLLY GOLLY GEE.
C7
B7
E7
E7
Am
WHO DO YOU BELIEVE'S TO BLAME FOR THAT? AND WHEN HE MUST UN- ZIP HIS
NOBODY TO BLAME BUT YOU KNOW WHO. AND WHEN HE SHOWS THE BOSS- 'S
WHAT'S HE DOING OUT THERE BY THAT TREE? AND WHEN HE WANTS TO TELL YOUR
Am
D7
D7
B7
ZIP- PER SO THAT GRAND- MA CAN MEET FLIP- PER, JUST RE- MEM- BER THAT
DAUGHTER HOW TO CUT ONE UN- DER WA- TER, JUST RE- MEM- BER THAT
EX- WIFE ALL THE DE- TAILS OF YOUR SEX LIFE, JUST RE- MEM- BER, RE-

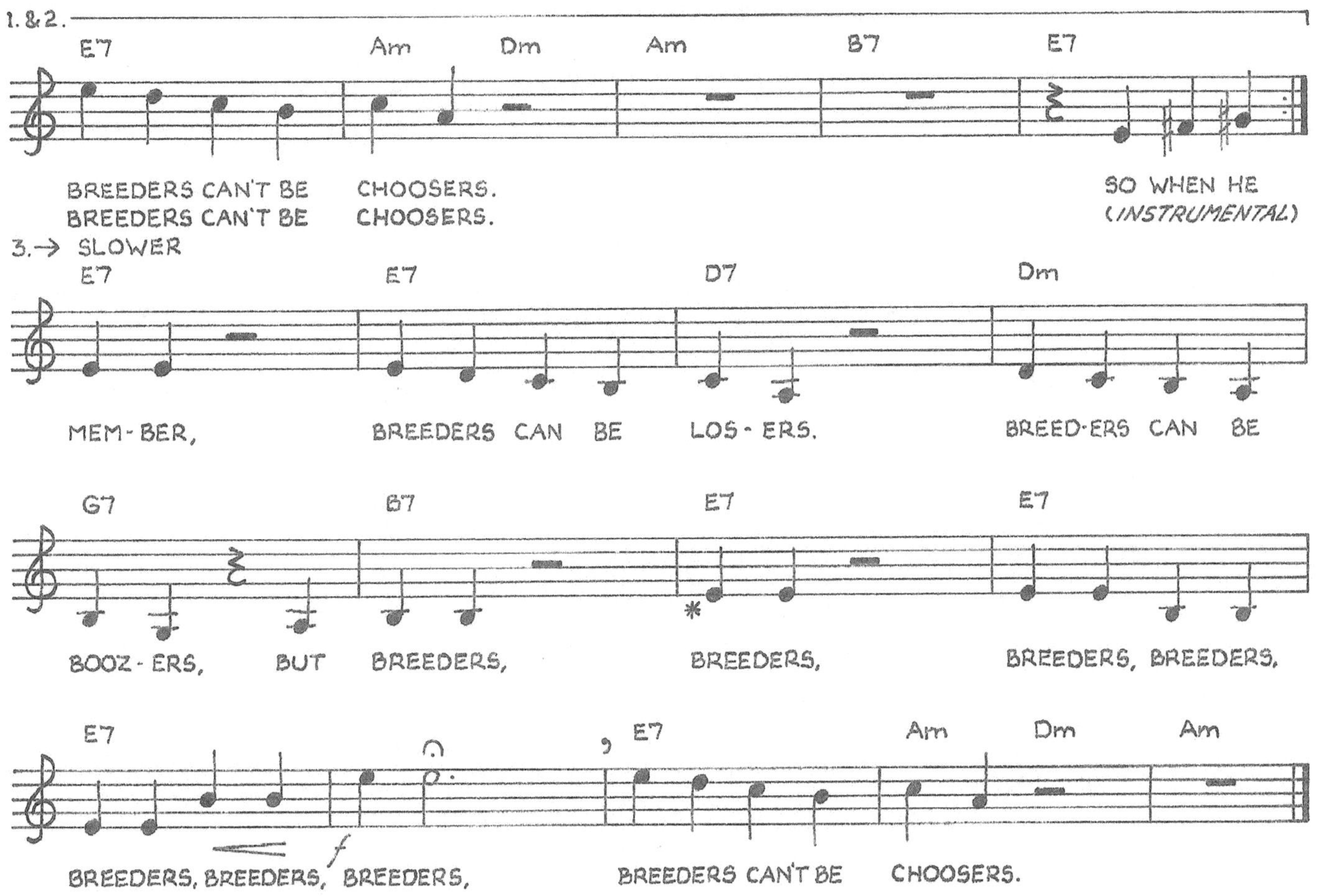
1. & 2.
E7 Am Dm Am B7 E7
BREEDERS CAN'T BE CHOOSERS. SO WHEN HE
BREEDERS CAN'T BE CHOOSERS. (INSTRUMENTAL)
3.→ SLOWER
E7 E7 D7 Dm
MEM-BER, BREEDERS CAN BE LOS-ERS. BREED-ERS CAN BE
G7 B7 E7 E7
BOOZ-ERS, BUT BREEDERS, BREEDERS, BREEDERS, BREEDERS,
E7 E7 Am Dm Am
BREEDERS, BREEDERS, BREEDERS, BREEDERS CAN'T BE CHOOSERS.

* AN OCTAVE LOWER, IF POSSIBLE

APRIL 2007
N.Y.C.

Buenas Noches, Little Roaches

FREELY
C E7 F A7 Dm7 G7 G7aug
mp
p
THE
C C♯dim7 Dm7 G7 C Am
SUN IS GO- ING DOWN, AND ALL O- VER TOWN EVE-RY-ONE IS HEAD-ING FOR THE
Dm G7 C C7 F Fm6
PIL- LOW AND THE SHEET. BUT IN THE KITCHEN THERE'S A STIRRING, THERE'S A CLICKING AND A WHIRRING, AND A
Dm7 G G7aug C E7
mp
PIT- TER PIT- TER PAT OF LIT- TLE FEET. BUE- NAS NOCH- ES, LIT- TLE
F A7 Dm G7 C Gdim7 G7
ROACH- ES. AS THE SUN SINKS IN THE WEST, IT'S TIME TO SCURRY FROM YOUR NEST. FOR NIGHT AP-
C C7 F F♯dim7 G7
PROACH- ES FOR LIT- TLE ROACH- ES, AND NIGHT- TIME IS THE TIME YOU LIKE THE
C E7 Am E7 Am E7
BEST. THE PEO- PLE ARE ALL SLEEP- ING, SO IT'S TIME TO COME A- CREEP- ING AND TO

F Dm G7 C E7 Am E7
NIB-BLE ON A COOK-IE AND SOME JUICE. BE-FORE THE SCRAPS ARE DRIED OUT, TIME TO
Am E7 D7 G7
SCAMPER FROM YOUR HIDEOUT, AND TO MEET AND GREET AND EAT AND RE-PRO- DUCE. SO BUE-NAS
C E7 F A7 Dm G7
NOCH- ES, LITTLE ROACH-ES. COME AND WAVE AT MIS-TER MOON AND LICK THE
C C♯dim7 G7 C C7 F F♯dim7
FROST-ING FROM THE SPOON. FOR NIGHT AP- PROACH-ES FOR LIT-TLE ROACH-ES, AND
G7 C C7 F F♯dim7
MOR-NING WILL BE COM- ING ALL TOO SOON. THE SANDMAN WATCHES O- VER CU- CA-
C C♯dim7 Dm G7 C C7
RA- CHAS. SO BUE-NAS NOCH- ES, MY LIT- TLE ROACH- ES. BUEN A- PE-
F Fm C C♯dim7 Dm G7 3 C
TI- TO, DEN CUENTA DEL BUR-RI- TO. HERMOSOS SUEÑOS, IN-SECTOS PE-QUE-ÑOS

NOVEMBER 1999 · N.Y.C

CAREERS

FAST
C
(NO CHORD)
f
f
1. WHEN I GROW UP I'M GON-NA BE A MONK,
SIT-TIN' IN A CELL WHILE I CHANT MY CHANTS. I'LL STUDY THE DI-VINE, AND
DRINK A LOT OF WINE, AND EAT A LOT OF BREAD, AND NEVER WEAR PANTS.

2. WHEN I GROW UP I'M GONNA BE A NEWSDEALER,
RINGIN' UP THE CHANGE WITH A DING DING DONG.
I'LL PEDDLE ALL MY SMUT
WHILE SITTIN' ON MY BUTT
AND YAKKIN' ON THE TELEPHONE ALL DAY LONG.

3. WHEN I GROW UP I'M GONNA BE A TRANSLATOR,
WRITIN' MY COPY WITH SAVOIR FAIRE.
I'LL POLISH OFF A TEXT,
AND THEN I'LL DO THE NEXT,
AND IF I GET A WORD WRONG NOBODY'LL CARE.

4. WHEN I GROW UP I'M GONNA BE A BARTENDER,
POURIN' OUT THE BOOZE LIKE A BUCCANEER.
IF SOMEONE'S IN A FUNK,
I'LL GET HIM GOOD AND DRUNK,
AND KNOCK HIM ON THE FLOOR, AND FINISH HIS BEER.

5. WHEN I GROW UP I'M GONNA BE A DOG GROOMER,
TRIMMIN' ALL THE POODLES THAT YAP YAP YAP.
I'LL GIVE 'EM ALL A BUZZ,
AND SWEEP AWAY THE FUZZ,
AND THEN I'LL HAVE A SANDWICH AND MAYBE TAKE A NAP.

6. WHEN I GROW UP I'M GONNA BE A BANK ROBBER,
HAULIN' OUT THE CURRENCY IN GREAT BIG SACKS.
I'LL COUNT UP ALL THE LOOT,
AND GO AND BUY A SUIT,
AND RUN AWAY TO FLORIDA AND SIT AND RELAX.

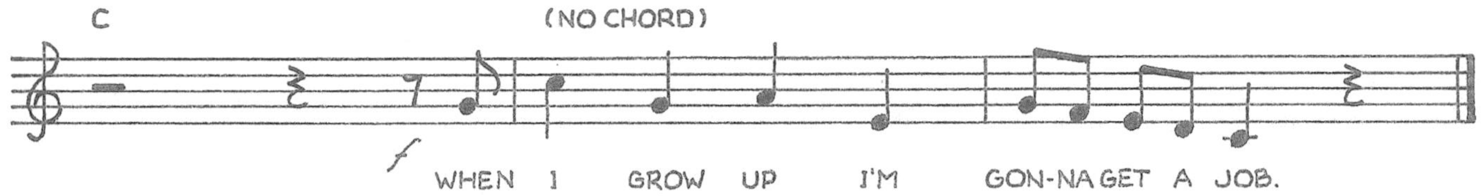
C
(NO CHORD)
f
WHEN I GROW UP I'M GON-NA GET A JOB.

JANUARY 1998
N.Y.C.

THE DEATH OF ORPHEUS

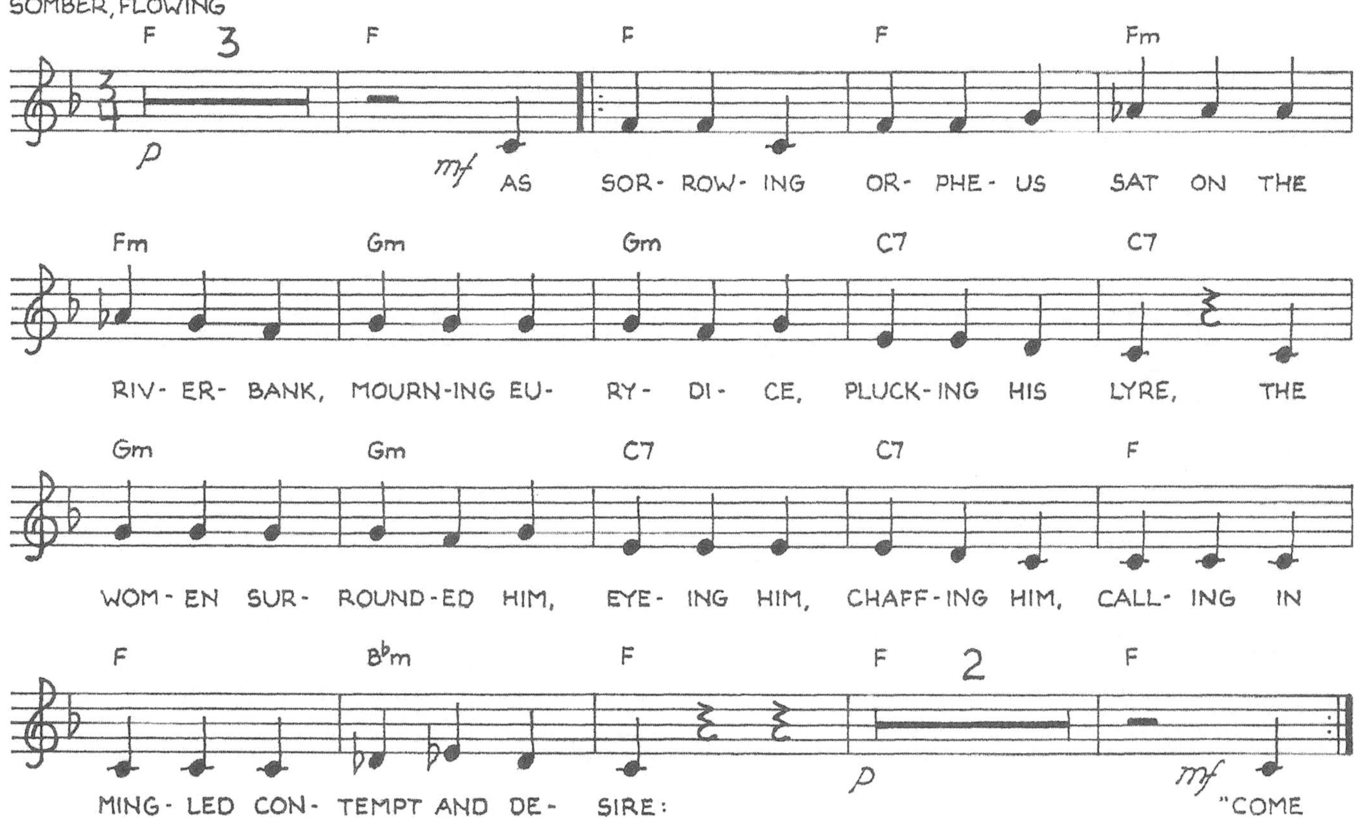
SOMBER, FLOWING
F F F F Fm
AS SOR- ROW- ING OR- PHE- US SAT ON THE
Fm Gm Gm C7 C7
RIV- ER- BANK, MOURN-ING EU- RY- DI- CE, PLUCK-ING HIS LYRE, THE
Gm Gm C7 C7 F
WOM- EN SUR- ROUND-ED HIM, EYE- ING HIM, CHAFF-ING HIM, CALL- ING IN
F B♭m F F F
MING- LED CON- TEMPT AND DE- SIRE: "COME

2. "COME PLAY WITH US, PRETTY BOY; THROW DOWN YOUR INSTRUMENT;
   LEAVE YOUR LAMENTS FOR THE JOYS OF THE FLESH."
   BUT NONE OF THEIR TAUNTS INTERRUPTED HIS MELODIES:
   ORPHEUS SANG, FOR HIS SORROW WAS FRESH.

3. THE WOMEN GREW ANGRY; THEIR BANTER GREW BITTERER;
   SOON THEY WERE HURLING ROCKS, BRICKBATS, AND TRASH.
   BUT ORPHEUS SANG IN A RING OF ENCHANTEDNESS;
   ALL OF THEIR ARSENAL POWDERED TO ASH.

4. THEY HOWLED EVER LOUDER, AND SO OVERPOWERED HIM,
   DROWNING THE SPELL OF HIS SONG WITH THEIR SCREAMS.
   THEY FELL ON HIM, SLAUGHTERED HIM, SLASHED AND DISMEMBERED HIM,
   SCATTERED HIS BITS TO THE RIVERS AND STREAMS.

FEBRUARY, 2011 - N.Y.C.

A MAN WHO HAS HIS HEAD UP HIS ASS HAS

A DIFFERENT POINT OF VIEW

SPIRITED
D F#m Bm G A7 D
Bm Bm Bm Bm Bm Em
SEE THAT MAN? IF HE CAN, HE'D
SEE THAT GUY? HE WILL TRY TO
F#7 Bm A7 D
LIKE TO PUT YOU DOWN. WHEN HE JEERS, DRY YOUR TEARS, AND
SHOW- ER YOU WITH SCORN. WHEN HE'S RUDE, DON'T YOU BROOD, AND
E7 A7 G A7
WIPE A- WAY THAT FROWN. IT HELPS, AS A MATTER OF COURSE,
DON'T YOU FEEL FOR- LORN. IT'S EA- SY TO FIGURE OUT WHY
E7 A7 E7 A7
TO CONSIDER THE SOURCE. FOR A
YOU DON'T SEE EYE TO EYE. FOR A
D F#m Bm G A7 D
MAN WHO HAS HIS HEAD UP HIS ASS HAS A DIFFERENT POINT OF VIEW. AND
MAN WHO HAS HIS HEAD UP HIS ASS HAS A DIFFERENT POINT OF VIEW. AND
A7 D G A7
IT SHOULD NOT SUR- PRISE YOU, IF HE SHOULD CRIT- I- CIZE YOU. FOR A
IT IS NOT OB- JEC- TIVE, BUT BASED ON HIS PER- SPEC- TIVE. FOR A

D F♯m Bm G A7 D
MAN WHO HAS HIS HEAD UP HIS ASS HAS A DIFFERENT POINT OF VIEW. THE
MAN WHO HAS HIS HEAD UP HIS ASS HAS A DIFFERENT POINT OF VIEW. TO
F♯7 Bm Em B7
REST OF THE HU- MAN RACE SEES THE WORLD AS A LAR - GER PLACE. WE CAN
US EVERYTHING LOOKS FINE, FOR WE DON'T HAVE A TWIS - TED SPINE. BUT THE
Em B7 Em B7 Em B7 E7
FEAST OUR EYES ON THE LOWS AND HIGHS OF THE SEAS AND SKIES, AND LOOK OUR NEIGHBOR IN THE
SCOFF - ING SCHMUCK HAS HIS VIEWPOINT STUCK IN THE MURK AND MUCK DOWN THERE WHERE THE SUN DOESN'T
A7 D F♯m Bm G A7
FACE. BUT A MAN WHO HAS HIS HEAD UP HIS ASS HAS A DIFFERENT VIEW THAN
SHINE. FOR A MAN WHO HAS HIS HEAD UP HIS ASS HAS A DIFFERENT VIEW THAN
G A7 G A7 G A7 G A7
ME OR YOU, AND I GUESS IN A WAY IT'S EQUAL - LY TRUE: IT'S A DIFFERENT POINT OF
ME OR YOU, AND YOU HAVE TO AD - MIT IT'S NARROWER TOO: IT'S A DIFFERENT POINT OF
D
VIEW.
VIEW.

DECEMBER 2015
HIGHLAND, N.Y.

Don't Despair

SLOW AND HEARTFELT
F C F C F C
mp mp
IF LOVE FAILS, TRY FRIENDSHIP. IF
A7 D B♭7 A7
FRIENDSHIP FAILS, TRY IN-DIFFERENCE. IF THAT FAILS, TRY HATE. AND IF
F♯dim7 A♭7 G7 C7 C7
HATE FAILS, AS IT OF-TEN DOES, DON'T DESPAIR, DON'T DESPAIR. IF
F C A7 D
HATE FAILS, TRY ANGER. IF ANGER FAILS, TRY HYP- NOSIS. IF
B♭7 A7 F♯dim7 A♭7 G7
THAT FAILS, TRY REST. AND IF REST FAILS, AS IT OF-TEN DOES,
C7 C7 F C
mf
DON'T DESPAIR, DON'T DESPAIR. GO WALK IN THE PARK, AND PICK UP A
F A7 D Gm
STICK, WASH YOUR HANDS, HAVE A SNACK. GO STAND ON A
Dm Gm Dm Gm
CLIFF AND SPIT IN THE SEA, WATCH THE SKY, WATCH YOUR BACK.

D7
G
D
B♭7
mp
IF REST FAILS, TRY MORE REST
IF MORE REST FAILS, TRY
E
C7
B♭7
G♯dim7
ST. JOHN'S WORT. IF THAT FAILS, TRY LOVE.
AND IF LOVE FAILS, AS IT
B♭7
A7
Gm7
C7
F
p
OF-TEN DOES, DON'T DE- SPAIR.

APRIL 1998
LOS ANGELES

Don't Talk to Me

FREELY
G7 C Cmaj7 Am D7
DON'T TALK TO ME. I DON'T WANT TO HEAR YOUR STORY.
DON'T TALK TO ME, I'M NOT GOING TO HELP YOU NETWORK.
D7 A♭7 G7 A♭7 G7
I DON'T WANT TO HEAR THE THINGS THAT YOU'VE DONE, ALL THE PRIZ- ES YOU'VE WON, AND
I'M NOT GOING TO TAKE YOUR CARD JUST IN CASE, I'M FOR-GET-TING YOUR FACE, FOR
F F♯dim7 C C♯dim7 G7 C7 E7
HOW YOU REACH THE TOP IN EACH AND EVE- RY CAT- E- GO- RY. NO NO NO
I'M IN-DIFFERENT AS TO IF YOU LIVE OR DIE OR GET WORK
F Fm C C7 E7
NO, I DON'T WANT TO SEE YOUR PRECIOUS BA- BIES. NO NO NO
NO, I DON'T WANT TO HEAR ABOUT YOUR SCREENPLAY. NO NO NO
F Fm C C7 E7
NO, I DON'T WANT TO HEAR HOW YOU GOT SCA- BIES. NO NO NO
NO, DON'T DESCRIBE THE TIME THAT YOU HEARD QUEEN PLAY. NO NO NO
F E7 Am Am
NO, I DON'T WANT TO FEED YOUR E- GO. AND SO IF
NO, I CAN GET MY OWN DAMN RE- FILL. IF YOU DON'T
D7 G7 G7 C Cmaj7
YOU TALK, ME GO. DON'T TALK TO ME.
BACK OFF, ME KILL. DON'T TALK TO ME.

Am
D7
D7
I'M NOT IN- TERESTED IN JE- SUS.
I DON'T WANT TO PLAY FLIR-TA- TION.
I DON'T WANT TO HEAR YOU
I DON'T WANT TO PROP YOUR
A♭7 G7 A♭7 G7 F F♯dim7
PRAISING THE LORD, I WOULD GET VERY BORED. JUST SHOW ME SCRIPTURE AND I'LL RIP IT
SAGGING ES-TEEM, AND TO NURTURE YOUR DREAM THAT YOU'RE NOT BLAND AND BORING AND UN-
C C♯dim7 G7 G7 C Cmaj7 Am D7
mp
IN- TO TI- NY PIEC- ES. DON'T TALK TO ME, DON'T TALK TO ME,
HINGED BY YOUR FRUSTRATION.
D7 A♭7 G7 A♭7 G7 C G7 C
p
DON'T TALK TO ME, DON'T TALK TO ME, DON'T TALK TO ME, DON'T TALK TO ME.

JUNE 2005 - N.Y.C.

FA LA LA LA LA

GRAVELY
Am Em F Em Dm G7 Am Dm E7
mf
mp
LIFE IS
Am Em F Em Dm G7
NAS- TY, IT IS BRUT- ISH, SAT-IS-FAC- TION'S IN AB- SEN-TI-A. WE SPEND YEARS IN DIS-AP-
Am Dm E7 Am Em
POINT- MENT AND IN- VID-I-OUS COM- PAR-I-SON. WE GROW OLD-ER, WE GROW WEAK- ER, WE GET
F Em Dm G7 Am Dm E7
CAN- CER AND DE- MEN-TI-A. THEN WE DIE AND THAT'S THE END OF US, LIKE WIL-LIAM HEN- RY
Am Am Em F Em
HAR-RI-SON. HE'S THE ONE WHO NAT-TERED ON SO IN THE RAIN AT HIS IN- AU-GU-RAL, CAUGHT PNEU-
Dm G7 Am Dm E7 Am
MO- NIA AND IT KILLED HIM AF-TER ON- LY A MONTH AS PRESIDENT. LIFE IS GIB- BER- ISH IN-
Em F Em Dm G7 Am
CAR- NATE, IT'S A CAV- AL-CADE OF DOGGEREL. IT'S A TALE TOLD BY AN ID-I- OT LIKE
Dm E7 Am F D7
f
WILLIAM HEN- RY HARRISON. FA LA LA LA LA, FA LA LA LA LA, FA LA

Gm A7 Dm E7 Am
LA LA LA, FA LA LA LA LA, FA LA LA LA LA. WE DON'T LIKE IT, WE RE-
mp
Em F Em Dm G7 Am
SIST IT, BUT WE KOW- TOW TO THE REG-I-MEN. THEN WE DIE AND THAT'S THE END OF US, LIKE
Dm E7 Am Dm E7 A Dm Am F
WILLIAM HEN- RY HARRISON'S GRANDSON BENJAMIN. FA LA LA LA LA,
f
D7 Gm A7 Dm E7 Am
FA LA LA LA LA, FA LA LA LA LA, FA LA LA LA LA.

OCTOBER 2009 - N.Y.C.

A Few Essential Principles

STAUNCH AND STURDY
C G C G F Gsus4 G
f
mf
OUR
C G F C F G
COUN- TRY IS BASED ON A FEW ESSENTIAL PRINCIPLES THAT GUIDE US SINCE WE'RE
SCI- ENCE AND ART AND PHI- LOS- O- PHY AND PO- ET- RY WILL ON- LY MEET WITH
JUS- TICE AND TRUTH, AND DE - MOC- RA- CY AND LIB- ER- TY ARE JUST A LOT OF
C G7 Am Em F A7
BORN. THEY ARE GREED, FAM- I- LY, FUN- DA- MENTALI - SM,
SCORN. THEY'RE NOT GREED, FAM- I- LY, FUN- DA- MENTALI- SM,
CORN. THEY'RE NOT GREED, FAM- I- LY, FUN- DA- MENTALI- SM,
1, 2.
3.
D7 G7 C C F G7
mp
GUNS, AND PORN. SO PORN. GREED IS THE MOTOR THAT
GUNS, AND PORN. AND
GUNS, AND
C G7 C F G7 C
MAKES THINGS RUN. FAM- I- LY BREEDS CHEAP LA- BOR.
D7 G D G D7
FUN- DA- MENTALI- SM KEEPS US DUMB AND GUNS KEEP US WA- RY OF OUR
G7 C E7 F A7
mf
NEIGH- BOR AND PORN IS THE BEDROCK OF A- MER- I- CAN WEDLOCK THAT

Dm Fm G7 C G
KEEPS OUR CI- TI- ZENS NUMB. AND IF YOU SHOULD STRAY FROM THESE
F C F G C Am Em
FEW ES-SENT-IAL PRINCIPLES, YOU'LL ON- LY FEEL FOR- LORN. STICK WITH GREED, FAM-I-LY,
F A7 D7 G7 C
FUN-DA-MENTALI- SM, GUNS, AND PORN.

JULY 2014
N.Y.C.

FILM CREW

MODERATO, LIGHT AND FLOWING
F Gm7 F Gm7
mp
F Dm F
mp
THERE'S A FILM CREW ON MY CORNER BLOCKING OFF THE STREET, SO I CAN'T USE THE SIDEWALK TILL THE
I'VE DONE ALL MY ERRANDS AND I'D LIKE TO TAKE A BATH, BUT UGLY LITTLE MEN WITH HEADSETS
Am Dm Gm
FILMING IS COMPLETE. I CAN'T REACH MY APARTMENT; I'M BARRED FROM MY OWN DOOR. IT
COME TO BLOCK MY PATH. AN ACTOR IS E- MOTING, SO I MUST NOT DISTURB. I
B♭ C7 B♭
LOOKS LIKE I'LL BE STANDING HERE AN- OTHER HOUR OR MORE. I PAY RENT ON MY
SHIFT MY HEAVY PACKAGES AND SIT DOWN ON THE CURB. LIFE IS HARD WHEN YOUR
Am B♭ C7 Am
A- PART- MENT, AND I'M DIS- CON- TENTED THAT I CAN'T GO THERE. THE
WAY IS BARRED BY A CROSS- ING GUARD WHO SAYS YOU CAN'T GO THERE. THE
Gm C7 A7 Dm Gm
CREW IS GETTING NERVOUS KEEPING HOMELESS PEOPLE OFF CRAFT SERVICE, BUT I AM GETTING
CREW MAY SHORTLY GO NUTS KEEPING HOMELESS PEOPLE OFF THE DONUTS, BUT I AM GOING
p
Gm C7 Gm C7 F
mp
NO- WHERE. THERE'S A FILM CREW ON MY CORNER,
NO- WHERE. SOMEDAY YOU MAY SEE THIS MOVIE

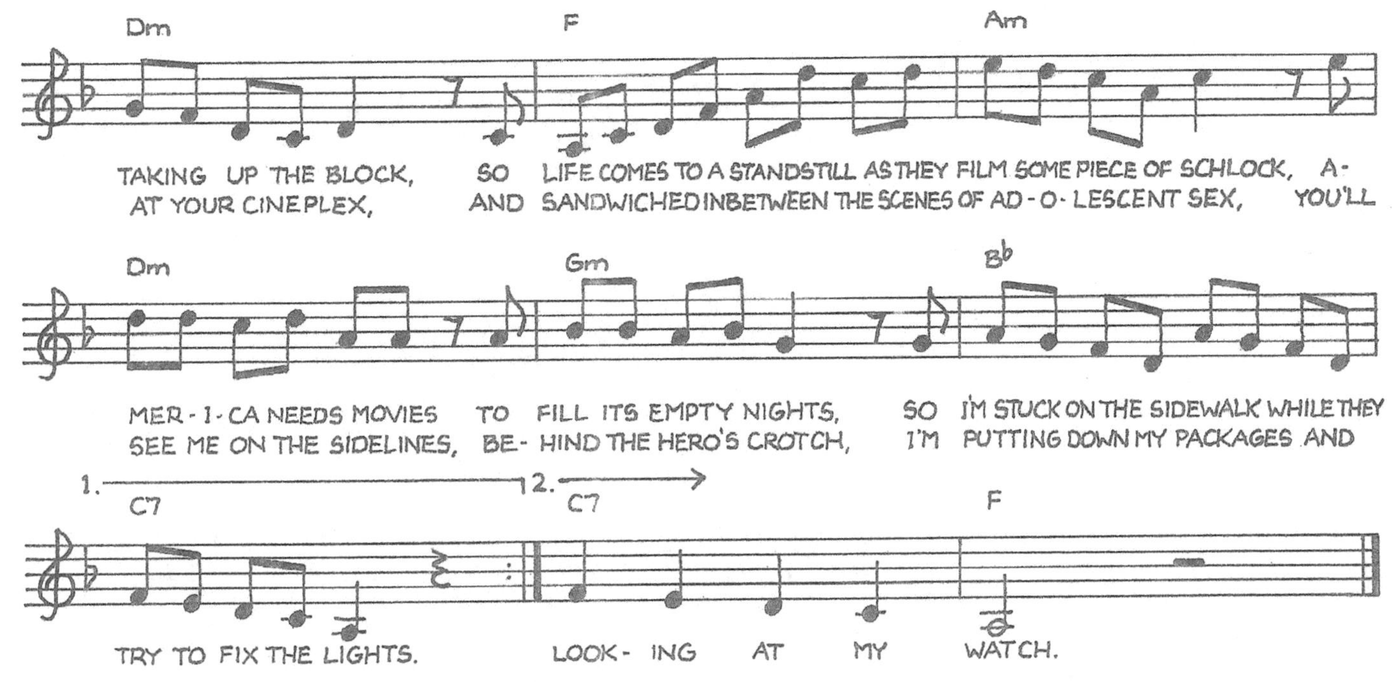
Dm
F
Am
TAKING UP THE BLOCK, SO LIFE COMES TO A STANDSTILL AS THEY FILM SOME PIECE OF SCHLOCK, A-
AT YOUR CINEPLEX, AND SANDWICHED INBETWEEN THE SCENES OF AD - O - LESCENT SEX, YOU'LL
Dm
Gm
B♭
MER - I - CA NEEDS MOVIES TO FILL ITS EMPTY NIGHTS, SO I'M STUCK ON THE SIDEWALK WHILE THEY
SEE ME ON THE SIDELINES, BE- HIND THE HERO'S CROTCH, I'M PUTTING DOWN MY PACKAGES AND
1.
2.
C7
C7
F
TRY TO FIX THE LIGHTS.
LOOK- ING AT MY WATCH.

JANUARY 1999
N.Y.C.

FLAKE FOOD

LIGHT AND UNHURRIED
A A A
p mf
AN OLD WOM- AN WHO HAD TROPICAL FISH
AN OLD MAN WHO HAD A PAPERBACK BOOK
D A B7 E7
SAT IN THE HOUSE ON A SUNNY AFTERNOON. SHE ATE HER LUNCH AND SHE
SAT IN THE PARK ON A SUNNY AFTERNOON. HE READ A LOT OF THE
B7 E7 D A F#m
mp
DRANK SOME PUNCH, WHICH THE FISH DIDN'T WANT. FISH DON'T WANT
NOV- EL'S PLOT, WHICH THE FISH DIDN'T WANT.
F#m C#m7 F#m C#m7
AN- Y- THING BUT FLAKE FOOD. FLAKE FOOD COMES FIRST.
F#m F#m C#m7 (NO CHORD)
mf
BE CARE- FUL YOU DON'T O- VER- FEED THEM. THE
A A D
OLD WOM - AN TOOK A WALK IN THE PARK, AND SAT ON A BENCH BY THE
A B7 E7 B7 E7
MAN WHO HAD THE BOOK. SHE WATCHED THE BIRDS, AND HE READ MORE WORDS, WHICH THE

D A A F#m
FISH DIDN'T WANT. THE CLOUDS THEN BE-GAN TO
F#m C#m F#m
FORM IN THE SKY. THE MAN WALKED A-WAY, AND THE WOMAN TOOK A BUS, SO THEY
F#7 Bm F#7 Bm B7
NEV- ER MET, AT LEAST NOT YET, BUT THE FISH DIDN'T CARE, THEY
B7 Bm E7 Bm E7
WEREN'T E- VEN THERE, THEY WERE EATING THEIR FLAKES IN THE TANK BY THE CHAIR.
Bm E7 F#m F#m C#m
mp
FISH DON'T WANT AN- Y- THING BUT FLAKE FOOD.
F#m C#m F#m F#m
FLAKE FOOD COMES FIRST. BE CARE-FUL YOU DON'T O- VER-
C#m C#7 F#m F#m
p
FEED THEM. THAT'S THE WORST.

MARCH 2000
LINCOLN, N.H.

GET ON THE GRID

RATHER BRISK
C C G7 G7 C C
p mp
1. GO FIND YOUR-SELF A JOB, AND
F G7 C C
EARN A MONTH-LY CHECK: GET ON THE GRID. SPEND
Am Am F G7
EVE- RY- THING YOU EARN ON FOOL- ISH- NESS AND DREK: GET ON THE GRID.
C C F C
THE PRI- CES JUST KEEP MOUN- TING; YOUR
G7 C F C
SAL- A- RY IS LOW. LET THEM DO THE AC- COUN- TING; JUST
Dm Dm Dm G7
GRAB YOUR CRED- IT CARD AND WAVE IT GAI- LY TO AND FRO. DON'T
Dm Dm Dm G7
FRET A- BOUT YOUR DEBT AND ALL THE MON- EY THAT YOU OWE:
G7 G7 G7 G7
YOU WOULD-N'T WANT TO KNOW. (AND)

2. AND WHEN YOU GET BACK HOME,
GET BUSY WITH YOUR BLOG:
GET ON THE GRID.
THOSE PICTURES OF YOUR BUTT
WILL SET THE WORLD AGOG:
GET ON THE GRID.
SPEND ALL NIGHT ON YOUR LAPTOP,
AND MILK YOUR SERVER DRY.
IF YOU POST LOTS OF CRAP, POP-
ULARITY WILL FOLLOW JUST AS SHIT ATTRACTS A FLY.
TELL ALL YOUR FRIENDS ON FACEBOOK ALL THE THINGS YOU LIKE TO BUY.
HI, EVERYBODY, HI!

3. AND IF YOU CHAT ENOUGH,
YOU'LL FIND YOURSELF A MATE:
GET ON THE GRID.
SEND IN YOUR FORM AND FEE,
CALL IN THE CHURCH AND STATE:
GET ON THE GRID.
THEN KEEP THOSE BABIES COMING;
MAKE CHILDREN BY THE SCORE.
THAT'S WHY YOU HAVE THAT PLUMBING:
REMEMBER WHAT YOUR PENIS AND YOUR UTERUS ARE FOR;
YOUR KEEPERS NEED EMPLOYEES AND CONSUMERS FOR THE STORE.
MORE, LITTLE MONKEYS, MORE!
AND...

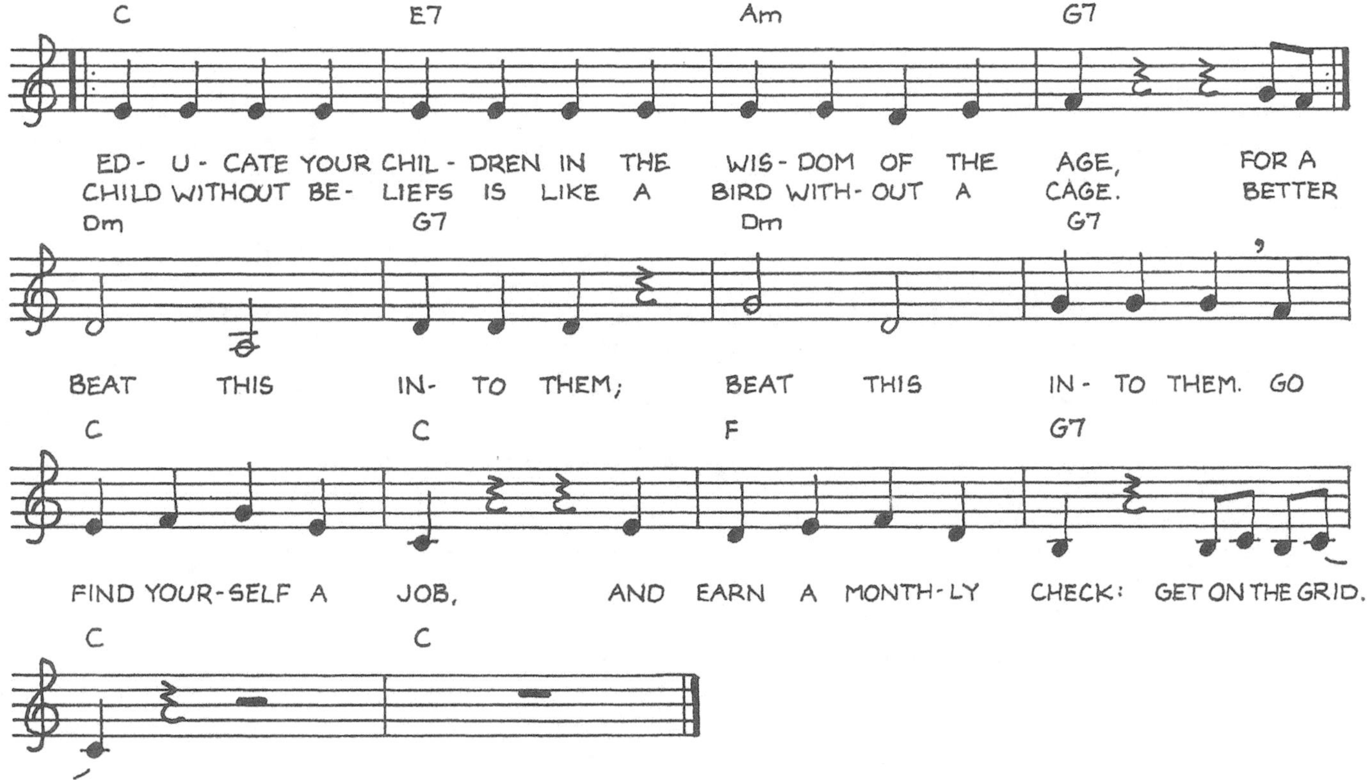
C E7 Am G7
ED- U- CATE YOUR CHIL- DREN IN THE WIS- DOM OF THE AGE, FOR A
CHILD WITHOUT BE- LIEFS IS LIKE A BIRD WITH- OUT A CAGE. BETTER
Dm G7 Dm G7
BEAT THIS IN- TO THEM; BEAT THIS IN- TO THEM. GO
C C F G7
FIND YOUR-SELF A JOB, AND EARN A MONTH-LY CHECK: GET ON THE GRID.
C C

MARCH 2008
N.Y.C.

Good Night

GENTLY ROCKING, NOT TOO SLOW
G Gmaj7 G6 Gmaj7 C Cmaj7 C6 Cmaj7
mp
G Gmaj7 G6 Gmaj7 Am7 D7 Am7 D7
G Bm Em A7 Am7 D7
p
DAY IS DONE. DROP YOUR CARES AND TUMBLE INTO BED.
G Em A7 Am7 D7
EVE- RY- ONE TURNS INTO A TI- NY SLEEPYHEAD. SLEEP KNITS
Gmaj7 B7 Em A7 Am7 D7
UP THE RAVELL'D SLEEVE OF CARE. SO TODDLE OFF TO BED AND NESTLE THERE. GOOD
mp
G Gmaj7 G6 Gmaj7 C Cmaj7
NIGHT. TIME TO SETTLE DOWN AND VEG- E- TATE,
C6 Cmaj7 Cm Cm/maj7 Cm6
FALL UNCONSCIOUS AND HALLU- CI- NATE. AND TO
G Bm E7 Am7 D7
HOPE THAT IN THAT HELP-LESS STATE, YOU WILL NOT BE ATTACKED AND YOUR

Am7 D7 G Gmaj7 G6 Gmaj7
HOME WON'T BE SACKED. GOOD NIGHT, SHUT YOUR WEARY EYES AND
C Cmaj7 C6 Cmaj7 Cm
START TO DROOL, TILL YOUR PILLOW'S LIKE A SWIM- MING POOL.
Cm/maj7 Cm6 G Bm E7
DON'T BE SCARED THAT YOU'LL LOOK LIKE A FOOL, FOR YOU'LL
Am7 D7 Am7 D7 Bm7
LOOK SO MUCH MORE WHEN YOU START IN TO SNORE. IT'S NA- TURE'S WAY THAT
E7 C B7 Em
WE SHOULD STAY A THIRD OF EACH DAY AS LIFE- LESS CLAY, SO
A7 Am7 D7 G Gmaj7
WHAT CAN WE SAY? WE HAVE TO O- BEY. GOOD NIGHT.
G6 Gmaj7 C Cmaj7 C6 Cmaj7
JUST PRETEND IT IS- N'T WAST- ED TIME, AS YOUR BRAIN SWIMS IN ITS
Cm Cm/maj7 Cm6 G Gmaj7 G6 Gmaj7
PSY-CHIC SLIME. GOOD NIGHT, GOOD

C
Cmaj7
C6
Cmaj7
G
Bm
E7
p
NIGHT,
GOOD
NIGHT,
GOOD
Am
Cm
G
Am7
D7
NIGHT,
GOOD
NIGHT,
GOOD
NIGHT,
GOOD
NIGHT,
GOOD
G
D7
Gmaj7
NIGHT,
GOOD
NIGHT.

MARCH 1988 - N.Y.C.

THE HYPNOTIST'S BIRTHDAY

LIVELY
D6→
mp
mf
IT'S THE HYPNOTIST'S BIRTH- DAY.
D6→
WHAT SHOULD WE GET HIM FOR A PRESENT? IT'S THE HYPNOTIST'S BIRTH- DAY.
D6→
F♯m
WHAT SHOULD WE GET HIM FOR A GIFT? HE AL- READY HAS A
G7
E7
A7
RECORD OF JAZZ, A SAX-O-PHONIST IM-PRO-VIS-ING ON OLD
G
A7
F♯m
POP TUNES. HE'S AL-READ-Y GOT A COL- LAPS-I- BLE COT, SO
A7
G
G♯
A7
D6
THAT WON'T DO. IT'S THE HYP-NO-TIST'S
D6→
BIRTH- DAY. WHAT SHOULD WE GET HIM FOR A BIRTH- DAY
D6→
PRESENT? IT'S THE HYP-NO-TIST'S BIRTH- DAY. WHAT SHOULD WE GET HIM FOR A

D6 F♯m G7
GIFT? HE AL-READY OWNS A BUCKET OF STONES. I
E7 A7 G A7
DON'T KNOW WHY HE HAS IT, BUT IT'S ON HIS BOOK-SHELF. HE'S
F♯m G7 A7
LOAD-ED WITH TIES, SO IT WOULDN'T BE WISE TO BUY A TIE.
G G♯ A7 D6→
IT'S THE HYP-NO-TIST'S BIRTH-DAY.
D6→
WHAT SHOULD WE GET HIM FOR A PRESENT? IT'S THE HYP-NO-TIST'S BIRTH-DAY.
D6→
WHAT SHOULD WE GET HIM FOR A BIRTH-DAY GIFT? WELL,
F♯m Em A7 D Ddim7 A7
WHAT ABOUT SOMETHING HE CAN USE IN HYP-NO-SIS? A MAG-IC WAND? HE
A7 Ddim7 A7 A7
DOESN'T USE THAT. A BOX OF CHALK? HE DOESN'T USE THAT.

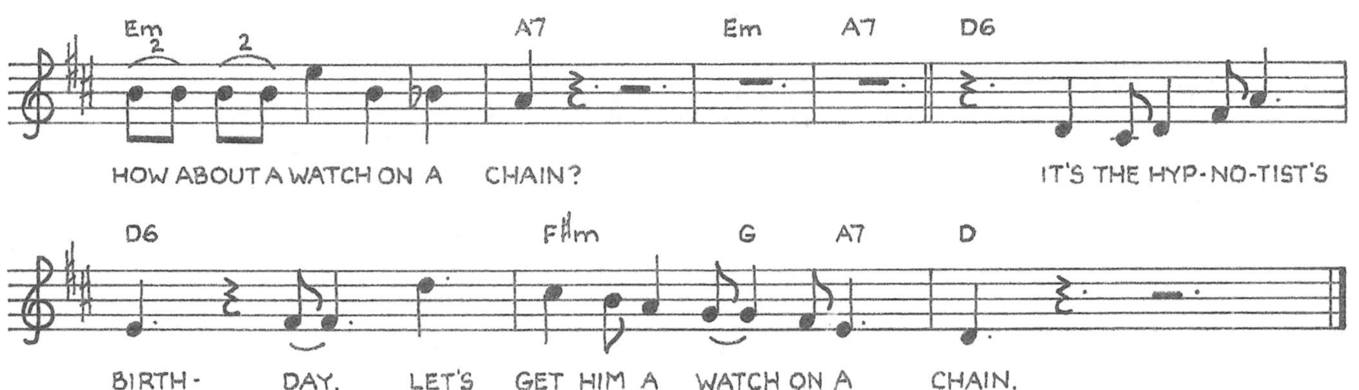
Em
A7
Em
A7
D6
HOW ABOUT A WATCH ON A CHAIN?
IT'S THE HYP-NO-TIST'S
D6
F♯m
G
A7
D
BIRTH- DAY. LET'S GET HIM A WATCH ON A CHAIN.

JULY 2000
BROOKLYN

I Just Don't Understand

SLOW AND EXPRESSIVE
B♭ Cm7 F7 B♭ Cm7 F7
mp mf
THINGS ARE SOMETIMES HARD TO FIGURE OUT. WE'RE
B♭ E♭m7 A♭7 Cm7 Gm7 Cm7
PARALYZED BY IGNORANCE AND DOUBT. IN THIS COCKEYED CARA- VAN THAT WE CALL
D♭9 Cm7 F7 Cm7 F7
LIFE, BECAUSE WE DON'T KNOW QUITE WHAT ELSE TO CALL IT. BUT
B♭ Cm7 F7 B♭
THERE'S ONE FACT OF WHICH I CAN BE SURE, ONE SHINING TRUTH I'M CERTAIN WILL EN-
E♭m A♭7 Dm7 Ddim7 Cm7 Cdim7
DURE. IT'S A LITTLE THING, NO MORE THAN A SEED, REALLY, BUT IT'S
Gm7 Gdim7 Cm7 F7
TRUE, AND I'D LIKE TO SHARE IT WITH YOU. I JUST DON'T
Cm7 F7 Cm7 F7
UN- DER- STAND THIS CHAIN OF PERPLEXING E- VENTS. I JUST DON'T
B♭maj7 E♭maj7 D7 Ddim7
UN- DER STAND, FOR IT DOESN'T BE-GIN TO MAKE SENSE. AND I'M

Cm7 D7 Gm D7 Ddim7
FOGGED AND BEFUDDLED, MY MIND IS ALL MUDDLED, I SIMPLY CAN'T FOLLOW THE BALL. FOR I JUST DON'T
Cm7 F7 Dm Ddim7
UN- DER- STAND ANYTHING AT ALL. I JUST DON'T
Cm7 F7 Cm7 F7
UN- DER- STAND. MY PUZZLE IS MISSING A PIECE. I JUST DON'T
B♭maj7 E♭maj7 D7 Ddim7
UN- DER- STAND, BUT I ACHE FOR THAT BLESSED RE- LEASE, FOR I'VE
Cm7 D7 Gm Ddim7
BATTERED AND BLED ON AND HAMMERED MY HEAD ON THAT BLANK AND UNBROACHABLE WALL, AND I JUST DON'T
Cm7 F7 Dm Ddim7
UN- DER- STAND ANYTHING AT ALL. NO, I JUST DON'T
Cm7 F7 A♭7 B♭maj7
UN- DER- STAND ANYTHING AT ALL, AT ALL.

AUGUST 1994
N.Y.C.

IF SOMETHING GOES WRONG, JUST PRETEND IT DIDN'T HAPPEN

CHEERFUL
Gm C7 F F♯dim7 Gm C7
mf f
IF SOMETHING GOES WRONG, JUST PRETEND IT DIDN'T HAPPEN, PRE-
Gm C7 F Dm C7 F F♯dim7 Gm C7
TEND IT DIDN'T HAPPEN, AND IT'LL GO A-WAY. IF SOMETHING GOES WRONG, JUST PRETEND IT DIDN'T HAPPEN, AND
Gm C7 Gm C7 F A7 (FINE) Dm Dm
mf mf
MAYBE YOU CAN DEAL WITH IT SOME OTHER DAY.
LET'S
LET'S
Dm Gm A7 Gm A7
SAY YOU'RE HAVING DINNER WITH A MIN-IS-TER OF STATE, A FOREIGN PO-TEN-TATE,
SAY YOU LOOK AROUND AND YOU'RE DISGUSTED AT THE SIGHT, COR-RUPTION'S AT ITS HEIGHT,
Cm F7 B♭ B♮dim7 A7
WOULDN'T THAT BE GREAT? DIS-CUSSING MARKET GOALS IN THE SA-HA-RA, WHEN
WRONG HAS CONQUERED RIGHT, AND EVE-RY-THING IS CHEAP AND VILE AND HO-KEY, SO
Dm Gm A7 G7 Gm7 C7
SUDDENLY HE SNEEZES AND EXPELS HIS UPPER PLATE RIGHT INTO HIS PASTA PRIMA-VE-RA.
DO YOU SPEAK YOUR MIND OR DO YOU TRY TO BE POLITE JUST PRETEND THAT ALL IS OKEY-DO-KEY?
Gm7 C7 G7 C7 G♯dim7 G♯dim7
HOW DO YOU RE-ACT WITH DIG-NI-TY AND TACT?
HOW DO YOU RE-ACT SO YOU WON'T BE AT-TACKED?

FEBRUARY 1995 - N.Y.C.

In Memoriam

LIGHT, BUT FUNEREAL
Am Dm Am G7 G7aug
f p
C C C♯dim7
mp
NOW THAT I AM DEAD, THEY GATHER BY THE BED TO SAY, "HE'S PASSED A-
ONCE I'M IN THE SACK, THEY DRAG ME OUT THE BACK, AND TUCK ME IN THE
Dm D7 Bm
WAY." THEY RI- FLE MY POCK- ETS AND THEY DIV- VY UP THE CHANGE. I
TRUCK. OUR NEW DES-TI- NA- TION IS THE UN- DER-TAK-ER MAN. I'D
Em D7 A7 D7 D7
FIND IT A BIT OF A SHOCK, IN FACT I FIND IT RATHER STRANGE. THEY
WANTED A SIMPLE CREMATION, BUT I GUESS THAT'S NOT THE PLAN. THEY
G G A7
HAVE A DRINK AND CHAT, THEN SOMEONE TAKES HIS HAT, AND STICKS IT ON MY HEAD AS A
STOP ALONG THE ROUTE, A SCHOOL HAS JUST LET OUT, THEY'D LIKE TO TRY TO MAKE THE KIDS
A7 E♭7 D7 E♭7 D7
GAG. THEY PROP ME UP FOR PHOTOGRAPHS, AND REALLY HAVE A LOAD O'LAUGHS, AND
SCREAM. THEY MAKE ME WALK LIKE DRACULA, THE KIDS THINK I'M SPECTACULAR, WHICH
G7 Dm7 G7 G7 1. G7aug
p
THEN IT'S TIME TO PUT ME IN THE BAG.
IS- N'T QUITE AS FUN AS IT MAY SEEM.

2.
E7 Am F Dm
mf
I DID NOT EX- PECT THIS SHOW OF UT- TER DIS- RE-
Am Em E7 Am
SPECT FROM FRIENDS AND FAM-I-LY. CUS- TOM STILL MAIN-
F Dm Am Em
TAINS THAT ONE SHOULD TREAT THOSE LAST RE- MAINS A BIT LESS HAM-MI-LY. IT'S
Edim7 D7 D7 G7
TRUE. BUT THERE'S NOT A LOT THAT I CAN DO.
E7 E7 A7 A7 A7aug
mf
p
D D D♯dim7
mp
PAINT-ED AND PRESERVED, MY LIPS BIZARRELY CURVED, I REST TO BE AS-
Em E7 C♯m
SESSED. THE SUIT THAT I'M WEAR-ING IS A WEATHERBEATEN PLAID. IT'S
F♯m E7 E7
SOMEWHAT IN NEED OF REPAIRING, BUT I GUESS IT'S ALL THEY HAD. A

A
A
B7
PREACHER NOW BEGINS TO I- TEM-IZE MY SINS, EX- PLAINING HOW THEY MAKE JE-SUS
B7
F♮7
E7
F♮7
HURT. TO FOLLOW THIS DEBACLE, WELL, THE ORGAN PLAYS SOME PACHELBEL, AND
A7
A7
Dm
Gm
mf
THEN THEY DROP THE COF-FIN IN THE DIRT. DUST UN- TO
Dm
Dm
Gm
Dm
Dm
Gm
DUST. ASH- ES TO ASH. WHY CAN'T THEY
Dm
Gm
Dm
Gm
A7
Dm
JUST SHOW A LIT- TLE MORE PA- NACHE?

MAY 1989
N.Y.C.

IT'S EASY TO BE AN ECCENTRIC NOWADAYS

LIGHT AND UNHURRIED
C F G C F G7
mp
mp
IT'S
C F C G C F A♭
EAS-Y TO BE AN EC- CENTRIC NOWADAYS. IT USED TO BE A FULL- TIME
EAS-Y TO BE AN EC- CENTRIC NOWADAYS. IT USED TO BE A DAUNT-ING
Gsus4 G7 Am7 F9 Dm B♭9
GIG. YOU HAD TO CLAIM THE EARTH WAS HOLLOW, BUILD A TEMPLE TO A- POL- LO, OR
TASK. YOU HAD TO KEEP AN AR-MA- DIL- LO, USE YOUR COFFIN AS A PIL- LOW, OR
A7 Dm A7 Dm A7 Dm
WEAR A BAG OF GARBAGE AS A WIG. THAT'S WHAT IT TOOK. BUT
NEVER LEAVE THE HOUSE WITHOUT A MASK. THAT'S WHAT YOU DID. BUT
C G7 C G7
NOW? JUST READ A BOOK. IT'S
NOW? DON'T HAVE A KID. JUST
B♭ A7 A♭ G C D7
DON'T ATTEND A CHURCH, DON'T BUY A LOT OF MERCH, RE- FUSE TO GET TAT-
G B♭ A7 A♭ G
TOOS. DON'T BUY THE LATEST PHONE, DON'T OP- ER-ATE A DRONE,

E♭ B♭ G G7 C F
DON'T HATE THE JEWS. IT'S EAS- Y TO BE AN EC-
C G C F A♭ Gsus4 G7
CENTRIC NOWADAYS. YOU USED TO HAVE TO WORK AT IT. YOU HAD TO
Am7 F9 Dm7 B♭9 A7 Dm A7
MEM-O-RIZE THE BI- BLE, SUE YOUR REL- A- TIVES FOR LI- BEL, OR SET UP YOUR A-PARTMENT IN A
Dm A7 Dm A7 Dm
PIT. YOU HAD TO HAVE A CER- TAIN TOUCH. BUT
C G7 3 C
NOW? IT DOESN'T TAKE MUCH.

MARCH 2017
NEW PALTZ, N.Y.

JAMES

MODERATO
G
D7
G
C
mp
mf
1. OH, EVERYBODY TALKS A-BOUT YOUR JE-SUS ALL THE TIME. THEY
D7
G C G
Em
TALK ABOUT HIS FATHER AND HIS MOTHER. AND THE SHEPHERDS IN THE FOLD, AND THE
A7
D7
G C G
MAGI WITH THE GOLD, BUT NO-ONE EVER TALKS ABOUT HIS BROTHER. LIT-TLE
Am
Cm
D7
G C G
JAMES CHRIST, LITTLE JIMMETY CHRIST. NOBODY CARES ABOUT JAMES. 2. HIS

2. HIS MOTHER SAID THAT JESUS WAS A MIGHTY KING OF KINGS;
HIS FATHER SAID THAT JESUS WAS THE SAVIOR.
BUT THE BROTHER WAS A KID
WHO NO MATTER WHAT HE DID
COULD NEVER MEASURE UP TO THAT BEHAVIOR.
LITTLE JAMES CHRIST, LITTLE JIMMETY CHRIST.
NOBODY CARES ABOUT JAMES.

3. NOW, JESUS CHANGED THE WATER INTO WINE, THE PEOPLE SAY,
IN HONOR OF A MERCHANT AND HIS DAUGHTER.
LITTLE JIMMY TRIED THE TRICK,
BUT HE COULDN'T MAKE IT STICK:
HE ONLY TURNED THE WATER INTO WATER.
LITTLE JAMES CHRIST, LITTLE JIMMETY CHRIST.
NOBODY CARES ABOUT JAMES.

4. AND JESUS FED THE MULTITUDE A PICNIC ON THE GRASS;
HE MULTIPLIED THE LITTLE LOAVES AND FISHES.
EVERYBODY ATE AND ATE,
EVERYBODY HEAPED HIS PLATE,
AND LITTLE JIMMY HAD TO DO THE DISHES.
LITTLE JAMES CHRIST, LITTLE JIMMETY CHRIST.
NOBODY CARES ABOUT JAMES.

5. AND JESUS GATHERED PEOPLE FOR A SERMON ON THE MOUNT,
AND HELD THEM ALL ENRAPTURED WITH HIS PREACHING.
LITTLE JIMMY ALSO WENT
AND SET UP A LITTLE TENT
BUT FOUND HE HAD NO TAKERS FOR HIS TEACHING.
LITTLE JAMES CHRIST, LITTLE JIMMETY CHRIST.
NOBODY CARES ABOUT JAMES.

G C D7
mf
6. THE ROMANS THOUGHT THAT JESUS WAS A DANGER TO THE STATE. THEY THOUGHT THAT HE WAS PLOTTING FOR THE
G C G Em A7
THRONE. SO THEY CRUCIFIED HIM HIGH: IT'S AN AWFUL WAY TO DIE. BUT THEY
rall.
D7 G C G Am
LEFT LITTLE JIMMY A- LONE. LITTLE JAMES CHRIST, LITTLE
Cm D7 G
JIM-ME-TY CHRIST. NOBODY CARES A- BOUT JAMES. LIT-TLE
Am Cm D7 G C G
JAMES CHRIST, LITTLE JIMMETY CHRIST. NOBODY CARES ABOUT JAMES.

JUNE 2014
NYC

Let the Patient Lift the Panniculus

MEASURED
B♭ Gm Dm Gm C7 F7
mf
mp
LET THE
B♭ Gm Dm D7 Gm C7 F7
PA- TIENT LIFT THE PAN- NICULUS. LET THE PA- TIENT LIFT THE FAT, FOR YOU
B♭ E♭ B♭ G7 Cm F7 B♭ F7
NEV- ER KNOW WHAT'S GROW- ING IN THAT FER- TILE HAB- I- TAT. A PHY-
B♭ Gm Dm D7 Gm C7 F7
SI- CIAN MUST BE ME- TIC-U-LOUS WHEN YOU START TO PROBE WITH- IN ALL THOSE
B♭ E♭ B♭ G7 Cm F7 B♭ B♭7
FOLDS OF FAT- TY TIS- SUE AND THOSE ROLLS OF STICK- Y SKIN. YOU WILL
mf
E♭ A♭ Fm B♭7 E♭ A♭ E♭ B♭7
FIND THINGS STRANGE AND RIDICULOUS, YOU WILL FIND THINGS NO ONE LOVES. AND YOU
E♭ G7 Cm F7 B♭ F7 B♭ B♭7
WILL NOT WANT TO TOUCH THEM, E- VEN WITH YOUR RUB- BER GLOVES. YOU MAY
E♭ A♭ Fm B♭7 E♭ A♭ E♭ B♭7
SEE SOME SORES, A PED- IC- U- LUS, OR A NEST OF LAR- VAL FLIES. AND YOU

E♭ G7 Cm F7 A♭ G7 Cm
MAY EN- COUN- TER FUN- GUS OF SUR- PRIS- ING SMELL AND SIZE. SO A-
mp
B♭ E♭ F7 B♭ Gm Dm D7
GAIN, I DO AD- VISE: LET THE PA- TIENT LIFT THE PAN- NICULUS WHEN YOU
Gm C7 F7 B♭ E♭ B♭ G7
GIVE HIM HIS EX- AM, FOR YOU NEV- ER KNOW WHAT'S HID- DEN IN THOSE
Cm F7 B♭
SLABS OF HU- MAN HAM.

JUNE 2001
NAPLES, MAINE

LET'S RIDICULE THE NIGHTINGALE

A GRACEFUL WALTZ
C E7 F C F D7 G7
mp
mf
LET'S
C E7 F C
RID - I - CULE THE NIGHTINGALE WHO WARBLES IN THE SHADE. HE
(INSTRUMENTAL)
F C D7 G7
DOES HIS WORK TO NO A- VAIL, FOR HE IS NEV- ER PAID. HE
C E7 F C
SER- E - NADES THE SET-TING SUN, UP IN THE WIL- LOW TREE. HE
F C G7 C
CAN'T GET PAID BY AN- Y- ONE; HE NEV-ER EARNS A FEE. THE
THE
A♭ C A♭ C
NIGHTINGALE CAN'T MON- E- TIZE HIS SIL-LY LIT- TLE SONG. AND
NIGHTINGALE CAN'T PAY HIS BILLS. THE NIGHTINGALE CAN'T SHOP. NO-
B7 Em G D7 G7
SO HE LIVES ON FLIES, AND THAT IS VER-Y WRONG.
BOD-Y BUYS HIS TRILLS. IT'S TIME FOR HIM TO STOP.

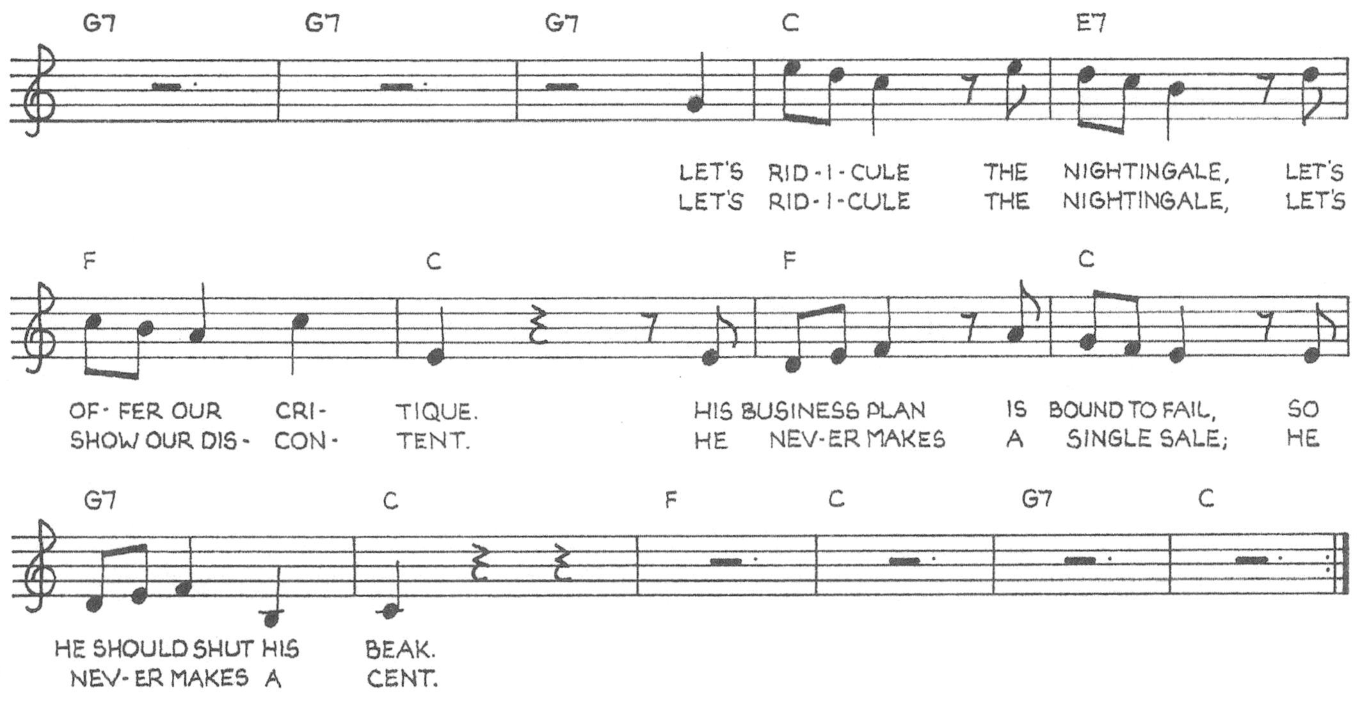
G7
G7
G7
C
E7
LET'S RID-I-CULE THE NIGHTINGALE, LET'S
LET'S RID-I-CULE THE NIGHTINGALE, LET'S
F
C
F
C
OF-FER OUR CRI- TIQUE.
SHOW OUR DIS- CON- TENT.
HIS BUSINESS PLAN IS BOUND TO FAIL, SO
HE NEV-ER MAKES A SINGLE SALE; HE
G7
C
F
C
G7
C
HE SHOULD SHUT HIS BEAK.
NEV-ER MAKES A CENT.

JULY 2014 - N.Y.C.

LITTLE FLOWER

LIGHT AND LILTING
A Bm A Bm A Bm
p mp
PRETTY LITTLE FLOWER, FORGIVE YOUR UNCLE DOUG. I'M
A Bm G7 G7
SORRY THAT I KICKED YOU. I THOUGHT YOU WERE A SLUG. FOR-GIVE ME, LITTLE
A A C♯m7 F♯m
FLOWER. I'M SORRY, I'M SORRY, I'D LIKE TO TAKE IT BACK. I
C♯m7 F♯m G7 G7
SEE NOW THAT'S A BLOSSOM, AND NOT A MUCUS TRACK. FOR-GIVE ME, LITTLE
A A Dmaj7 Dm7
FLOWER. I WAS JUST MISTAKEN WHEN I STRUCK YOU WITH MY SHOE. I
Em Gm7 G7 G7
DIDN'T RECOGNIZE YOU IN THAT COAT OF CLAMMY DEW. FOR-GIVE ME, LITTLE
A A C♯m7 F♯m
FLOWER. I'M SORRY, I'M SORRY, IT HAPPENS ALL THE TIME. I
Bm C♯7 D B7 E7 Bm E7 G7
FAIL TO SEE THE BEAU-TY LY- ING UN- DER- NEATH THE SLIME.

G7
G7
G7
A
C#m7
p
LITTLE FLOWER.
I'M SORRY, I'M SORRY, I'M
C#m7
F#m
F#m
SORRY, I'M SORRY, FOR- GIVE ME, FORGIVE ME, FOR- GIVE ME, FORGIVE ME.

MARCH 1991 - N.Y.C.

LITTLE TWO-HEADED KITTEN

FREELY
Gm7 C7aug B♭maj7 Asus4 A7 Gm7
mf
WHEN YOU WERE BORN THAT MEM-O-RA-BLE MORN, YOU OPENED ONE EYE, AND THEN AN-
C7 Cm7 A♭9
OTH- ER, AND THEN AN- OTH- ER, AND THEN AN- OTH- ER, WHAT A SUR-
A♮m9 D7 Gm7 C A♭maj7 G7
PRISE ALL THOSE EYES WERE TO YOUR MOTH- ER. BUT SHE LOVED YOU ALL THE MORE, LITTLE
Gm7 C7aug Fmaj7 Gm Fm B♭7
IN- STANT EN- CORE. LITTLE TWO- HEAD- ED KIT- TEN,
D♭maj7 F7 Am D7 B♭m E♭7
I WON'T PICK YOU UP; I DON'T WANT TO BE BIT- TEN BY ALL THOSE TEETH THAT NATURE BE-
A♭maj7 E♮dim7 Fm B♭7 G♭9 F7sus4 F7aug
QUEATHED TO YOU. YOU HAVE QUITE A FEW, LITTLE TWO- HEADED KIT- TEN. OH, YOU
B♭maj7 F♯dim7 Gm E♭m Dm E♭m
HAVE ONE MOUTH TO BITE & CHEW AND THEN ONE MORE TO CRY & MEW. YOU TAKE YOUR PICK, YOU WON'T GET SICK IF YOU DO

Cm F7aug B♭maj7 F♯dim7 Gm E♭m
BOTH AT ONCE. YOU HAVE FOUR EYES TO LOOK AROUND, FOUR EARS TO PICK UP EVERY SOUND; YOU HAVE A
Dm A♭7 B♭7 E♭maj7 D♭maj7 D♭7 Gm C7
LOT. YOU'RE NOT JUST SOME ONE- HEADED KIT- TEN.
Fmaj7 Gm Fm B♭7 D♭maj7 F7
LITTLE TWO-HEADED KITTEN, WHEN I SAW YOUR FACES I WAS INSTANTLY
Am D7 Gm E♭7 F Dm G9
SMITTEN. I HOPE LIFE'S NOT TOO TOUGH WITH ALL THAT EXTRA STUFF. GOOD
Fmaj7 B♭9 Fmaj7 B♭9 Fmaj7
LUCK LITTLE KITTEN, GOOD LUCK LITTLE KITTEN, GOOD LUCK.

JULY 2000
BROOKLYN

Love Me Unconditionally

RATHER SLOW
A C♮7 Bm E7 A C♮7 Bm E7
mf
mp COME
Bm Dm A 3
TAKE ME BY THE HAND, FOR I AM YOURS TO HAVE AND TO
Adim7 C♯m C♮7 F♮ B♭7
CLUTCH. AND I WON'T ASK FOR MUCH
mf JUST
A C♮7 Bm E7 A C♮7 Bm E7
LOVE ME UN-CON-DI-TION-AL-LY.
mp YOUR
Bm Dm A 3
FRIENDS CAN BE DE- MAND- ING WITH THEIR OB- LI-GA-TIONS AND
Adim7 C♯m C♮7 F♮ B♭7
SUCH. BUT I WON'T ASK FOR MUCH:
mf JUST
A C♮7 Bm E7 A C♮7 Bm E7
LOVE ME UN-CON-DI-TION-AL-LY.
p I
F♮maj7 C♮m B♭maj7 E♭7 Dm B♭7
MAY BE CRAB-BY, OR COLD, OR SUR-LY, CAN-TAN-KER-OUS, OR

Am9 E♭maj7 B♭m A♭maj7 D♭7
DRUNK; OR RUDE, OR BOR-ING, OR MEAN, OR HY-PER, OR
Em G♮7 F♯7sus4 F♯7 Bm
IN A LIFE-LONG FUNK. SO STROKE MY FE-VERED
mp
Dm A Adim7
BROW, AND SOOTHE MY NERVES WITH YOUR TEN-DER TOUCH. AND
3
C♯m C♮7 F♮ B♭7 A C♮7
I WON'T ASK FOR MUCH: JUST LOVE
mf
Bm E7 A C♮7 Bm E7
ME UN-CON-DI-TION-AL-LY. JUST
A C♮7 Bm E7 A C♮7
LOVE ME UN-CON-DI-TION-AL-LY.
Bm E7 A Dm A
THAT'S ALL.

MAY 2000
BROOKLYN

Make a Wish

UNHURRIED
A A A A7
p mp
WHEN YOU SEE A HU- MAN BE- ING STANDING IN A DOORWAY PEEING,
WHEN YOU SPY A FRISKY RODENT FROLICKING WHERE RODENTS SHOULDN'T
A7 Bm E7
CLOSE YOUR EYES, AND MAKE A WISH. AND
CLOSE YOUR EYES, AND MAKE A WISH. AND
A A7 A7
WHEN IT SMELLS LIKE SOMETHING ROTTING, THEN YOU NO- TICE SOMEONE SQUATTING,
WHEN YOU NO- TICE LUST- Y WATERBUGS SPAWNING LOTS OF SON AND DAUGHTER BUGS,
Bm E7 F#m
CLOSE YOUR EYES, AND MAKE AN- OTH- ER WISH. WHEN THE WORLD IS CA- CA PEE- PEE,
CLOSE YOUR EYES, AND MAKE AN- OTH- ER WISH. WHEN THE WORLD IS FULL OF VER- MIN
Bm Bm Dm E7
DON'T GET SAD AND WEEPY, MAKE A HEART- FELT WISH. SO
THAT YOU CAN'T EXTERMI- NATE JUST MAKE A WISH. SO
A A7 A7
WHEN YOUR NEIGHBOR ON THE SUB- WAY SAT- IS- FIES HIM- SELF THE RUB WAY,
WHEN THE CRACKHEAD IN YOUR LOB- BY WANTS TO CHAT A- BOUT HIS HOB- BY,
Bm E7 A
CLOSE YOUR EYES, AND MAKE A WISH. AND WHEN YOU SPOT SOME LOWER FRAT FORM
CLOSE YOUR EYES, AND MAKE A WISH. AND WHEN YOU SEE YOUR LOCAL JUNK- IE

A7
A7
Bm
PUK-ING PITCHERS ON THE PLATFORM,
HEAVING UP SOME EX-TRA CHUNKY,
CLOSE YOUR EYES, AND MAKE A
CLOSE YOUR EYES, AND MAKE A
E7
F♯m
Bm
OTHER WISH. WHEN YOU FIND YOUR DAILY FARE RE-VEALS A WORLD THAT'S SCARY,
OTHER WISH. WHEN THE WORLD BECOMES TOO TOXIC, IT'S NOT PARADOX-I-
Bm
Dm
E7
Bm
MAKE A HEART-FELT WISH. WHEN THE WORLD IS GRIM AND VICIOUS,
CAL TO MAKE A WISH. WHEN THE WORLD IS GRIM AND VICIOUS,
mf
E7
Bm
E7
Bm
E7
Bm
E7
IT'S NOT SUPERSTITIOUS, IF YOU FILL YOUR HEART WITH WISH-ES, MAKE A WISH.
IT'S NOT SUPERSTITIOUS, IF YOU FILL YOUR HEART WITH WISH-ES, MAKE A WISH.
f
1.
2.
Bm
E7
Bm
E7
E7
A
MAKE A WISH, MAKE A WISH, SO MAKE A WISH.
MAKE A WISH, MAKE A WISH,

MAY 2004
N.Y.C.

MEDULLA OBLONGATA

LIGHT AND JAZZY
C7 C7 F6 Gm7
mf mf
IT'S YOUR ME-DUL-LA OB-LON-GA-TA. IT'S GOT A
(INSTRUMENTAL)
F6 C7 G♯dim7 Am
PILE OF CRUCIAL DA-TA. EVE-RY ACTION YOU TAKE, BOTH A-
G♮m A7 G7 E♭7 C7
SLEEP AND A- WAKE, IS ON FILE DEEP IN- SIDE. IT'S YOUR ME-
F6 Gm7 F6 C7
DUL- LA OB- LON- GA-TA. IT IS-N'T DEAD LIKE TERRA COTTA. IT'S A-
G♯dim7 Am G♮m A7 G7
LIVE AND IT'S CUTE, LIKE A FRESH LITTLE FRUIT IN YOUR HEAD.
E♭7 C7 D♭maj7 E♭7 Dm7 B♭7
OO LA LA! IT'S DE- LIGHT- FUL, IT'S DI- VINE.
LIFE WITH- OUT IT WOULD BE DULL.
(NO CHORD) B♭m7 Dm7 G7 Gdim7 G7 Gdim7
IT'S AT THE TOP OF THE SPINE. IT'S GOT A LOT OF FUNCTIONS THAT I
IT'S AT THE BACK OF YOUR SKULL. IT HELPS YOU WHEN YOU'RE STROLLING DOWN YOUR

G7 Gdim7 G7 Gm C7 C7aug
CAN'T EX- PLAIN. IT'S VER-Y NEC-ES-SAR-Y TO THE BASE OF THE BRAIN. IT'S YOUR ME-
LOV- ERS' LANE. IT'S VER-Y NEC-ES-SAR-Y TO THE BASE OF THE BRAIN. IT'S YOUR ME-
F6 Gm7 F6 C7
DUL-LA OB-LON-GA-TA. IT'S LIKE A NEU- RO- LOG- I-CAL PI- ÑA-TA.
DUL-LA OB-LON-GA-TA. IF YOU DON'T HAVE ONE, WELL, YOU REALLY OUGHTA.
F Cm F Cm F Cm F F Cm F Cm
p
M. E. D. U. L. L. A. O. B. L. O.
M. E. D. U. L. L. A. O. B. L. O.
F Cm F Cm F F♯dim7 G7
N. G. A. T. A. mf ME- DUL- LA OB- LON- GA- TA.
N. G. A. T. A. ME- DUL- LA OB- LON- GA- TA.
1.
Gm C7 Gm C7
HEY HEY HEY HEY HEY HEY HEY HEY
HEY HEY HEY HEY HEY HEY HEY HEY
2.
Gm Gm F♯dim7 G7
HEY HEY HEY HEY! ME- DUL- LA OB- LON- GA- TA.
Gm Gm Gm C7 F
HEY HEY HEY HEY ME- DUL- LA OBLONGA- TA.

SEPTEMBER 1996
N.Y.C.

MY FACE IS IN THE SAND

PLAINTIVE
I HAVE A LITTLE PIECE OF DRIFTWOOD HERE IN MY HAND. I'M
GOING TO DRAW A PICTURE OF MY- SELF IN THE SAND. SO WHEN THE PEOPLE COME TO
FROLIC AND TO SWIM, THEY'LL GAZE UPON MY FEATURES AND THEY'LL SAY LOOK AT HIM, LOOK AT
HIM. MY FACE IS IN THE SAND. EVERY-
ONE CAN SEE MY FACE AS LONG AS THE SAND HOLDS OUT, AND THERE'S PLEN-TY OF SAND BY THE
SEA. THEN TIME AND TIDE AND WIND AND RAIN WILL
ALL DO THEIR WORST. A JELLYFISH WILL DRIFT UP TO MY FACE AND THEN BURST. AND
KIDS WITH THEIR STICKS, AND DOGS WITH THEIR TRICKS, WILL SOON ERASE MY

Gsus4 G7 A♭ G7
FACE. AND I'LL HAVE TO DRAW THE PICTURE OVER A- GAIN. MY
Cm A♭ Gdim7
FACE IS IN THE SAND. EVE- RY- ONE CAN SEE MY FACE AS LONG AS THE
Fm B♭7 Fm B♭7 E♭ A♭ G
SAND HOLDS OUT, AND THERE'S PLEN- TY OF SAND BY THE SEA.

JANUARY 2000

My Pal Satan

ROUSING
E♭ C♭7 B♭7 E♭ C♭7 B♭7
f
E♭ D7 D♭maj7
mf
WHO'S THAT FEL- LA HOOFIN' DOWN THE STREET, A TIP- PY TIP-PI-TY TAPPIN' ON
C7 F7 C♭7 E♭
LIT- TLE GOAT FEET? IT'S MY PAL SA- TAN.
Fm B♭7 E♭ D7
WHAT A GUY! WHO'S THAT DAN- DY WITH THE HELL- FIRE TAN, A
D♭maj7 C7 F7 C♭7
COSMOPOLITAN VERSION OF THE GREAT GOD PAN? IT'S MY PAL
E♭ D7 Gm Cm D7
SA- TAN. HE'S NO GOOD - Y GOOD - Y NI- CEY
Gm G7 C7
NI- CEY. NO SIR! AND OH! THAT
C7 F7 B♭7
PE- NIS OF HIS IS I- CY. BRR BRR.

E♭
D7
D♭7
WHO'S THAT TEMPTER WITH THE HORN'S AND TAIL? WHO'S THE GUY TO SEE IF YOUR
C7
Fm
E♮7
E♭6
SOUL IS FOR SALE? IT'S MY PAL SA- TAN.
D7
G7
G7
C7
YOU CAN START HELL- CAT- TIN', IT'S NOT SO COM- PLEX.
C7
F7
F7
JUST START SCATTIN' SOME BACK- WARDS LAT- IN AND
B♭7
F7
Edim7
B♭7
B♭dim7
B♭7
DO- IN' SOME RIT- U-AL SEX. PAINT THAT STAR!
B♭dim7
B♭7
B♭dim7
B♭7
F7
B♭7
KILL THAT RAM! HAVE A LIT-TLE PAR-TY IN THE PEN- TA- GRAM.
B♭7
B♭7
B♭7
BROADER
E♭
DAMN DAMN DAMN, NON SER- VI- AM.
rall.
f
WHO'S THAT JOKER WITH THE
D7
D♭7
C7
RED- HOT GRIN? WHO'S THE DEVIL'S AD-VO-CATE FOR OLD-FASHIONED SIN? IT'S

Fm
E♮7
E♭9
B♭min7
E♭7
MY PAL SA- TAN. OLD
A♭
A♭m
Gm7
NICK, THE SER-PENT, BE- EL- ZE- BUB, THE FOUNDER AND DIRECTOR OF THE
C7
Fm
E♮7
E♭9
BRIMSTONE CLUB. IT'S MY PAL SA- TAN.
B♭m7
E♭7
A♭
A♭m
THE PRINCE OF DARKNESS, THE LORD OF FLIES. THAT
Gm7
C7
Fm
E♮7
OLD FALLEN ANGEL WITH THE MES-MERIZIN' EYES. IT'S MY PAL
Cm7
F7
Fm
E♮7
AND LET'S NOT KEEP HIM WAITIN', IT'S MY PAL
E♭
D6
E♭6
SA- TAN.

FEBRUARY 1990 - N.Y.C.

NOTARY PUBLICS

COOL AND RHYTHMIC

F9 F9 F9 F9
NOTARY
D♭7 F E♭7 D♭7
PUB- LICS HAVE GOT IT MADE. THEY SIT IN THE SHADE AND
F7 G♭7 G♮m7 C7 Gm7 C7 C♭7
SIP LEMON- ADE, AND ALL THEY'VE GOT TO DO IS STAMP A DOC - U - MENT OR TWO AND THEY GET
B♭9 G7 C7 F
PAID. I WANT TO BE A NO - TA - RY PUB - LIC. NOTARY
D♭7 F B♭7 D♭7
PUB - LICS DON'T HAVE TO SWEAT. THEY READ THE GA-ZETTE IN
F7 G♭7 G♮m7 C7 Gm7 C7 C♭7
THEIR KITCHENETTE. THEY STAMP SOME DOCUMENTS AND THEN THE CUSTOMER PRESENTS THEM WITH SOME
B♭9 G7 C7 F
PRESIDENTS. EARNIN' THEIR GRUB AS A NOTARY PUB - LIC. I
Gm7 F7 E♭7 B♭7 B♭m
HOPE SOME DAY THAT I CAN FOLLOW THEIR FOOT - STEPS. I KNOW THAT I WOULD BE A VER - Y

G7 Gm7 F7 E♭7
GOOD ONE. I DON'T KNOW HOW YOU GET THE CERTI-FI- CA- TION.
(NO CHORD) C7 D♭7 F
mp
NOTARY PUB- LICS DON'T FEEL THE CRUNCH. NO
E♭7 D♭7 F7 G♭7 G♮m7 C7
TIME CLOCK TO PUNCH, NO HO- UR FOR LUNCH. THEY O-PEN UP A SHOP AND THEN THE
Gm7 C7 C♭7 B♭9 G7
STACKS OF TWENTIES DROP IN BY THE BUNCH. I WANT TO BE EARNIN' MY
C7 F7 F7
p
FEE AS A NOTARY P. I
Gm7 F7 E♭7 B♭7 B♭m
WISH THAT I COULD FIND OUT HOW TO BECOME ONE. I WONDER IF YOU HAVE TO TAKE A
G7 (NO CHORD) C7 D♭7
mp
TEST FIRST. NOTARY PUB-LICS HAVE SAVOIR
F E♭7 D♭7 F7 G♭7
FAIRE. THEY LOUNGE IN A CHAIR IN THEIR UN-DER- WEAR. WHEN

Gm7
C7
Gm7
C7
C♭7
B♭7
DOCUMENTS NEED STAMPIN' THEN THEY JUST UNHOOK THE CLAMP AND STAMP IT THERE.
I'D BE SWIMMIN' IN
G7
C7
F
BUB- BLY
AS A NOTARY PUB - LI -
C.

OCTOBER 1998 - N.Y.C.

OH DEAR, OH DEAR
(MAMAN, MAMAN)

LILTING
Cmaj7 Cmaj7 Dm7 G7 Cmaj7 Cmaj7 Dm7 G7
p mp
OH
MA-
Cmaj7 Cmaj7 Em7 C♯dim7 Dm7
DEAR, OH DEAR, AN- OTH- ER YEAR, AND WE'RE ALL
MAN, MA- MAN, UN NOU- VEL AN, ET L'ON EST
G7 C C Dm7 G7
HERE A- GAIN. EARTH IS BE- GIN- NING THAT
PLAN- TÉ LÀ. NO- TRE PLA- NÈ- TE SE
Dm7 G7 C D7 Dm7
SAME ROUND OF SPIN- NING IT'S DONE SINCE WHO KNOWS WHEN.
TOUR- NE LA TÊ- TE EN- CORE UNE AU- TRE FOIS.
G7 B♭7 E♭maj7 G7 Cm
FROM SUM- MER TO FALL, FROM WIN- TER TO SPRING.
L'AU- TOM- NE, L'HI- VER, LE PRIN-TEMPS, L'É- TÉ.
D7 G7 A♭7 G7 Cmaj7
THIS YEAR WILL BRING US BACK THE WHOLE THING. AND YOU AND
LE DÉ- FI- LÉ VA RE- COM-MEN- CER. ET L'ON EST
C7 Fm6 Fm6 Cmaj7 G7
I ARE STILL HERE: OH DEAR, OH DEAR, OH
PLAN- TÉ DE- DANS: MA- MAN, MA- MAN, MA-
C C
DEAR.
MAN.
DECEMBER 2008 - N.Y.C.

Peepee Caca Fucky-Fuck

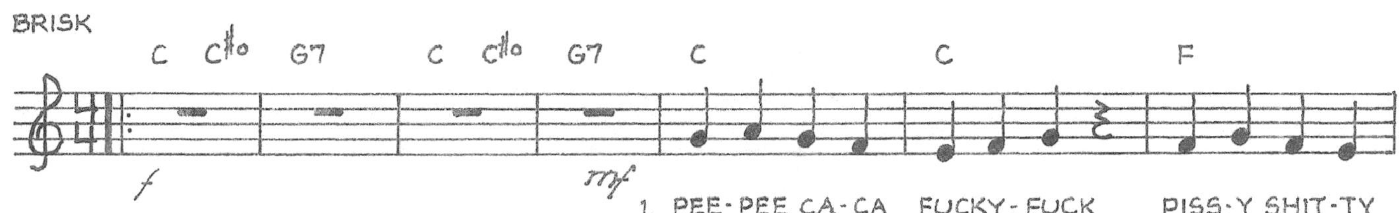
BRISK
C C♯o G7 C C♯o G7 C C F
f
mf
1. PEE-PEE CA-CA FUCKY-FUCK PISS-Y SHIT-TY

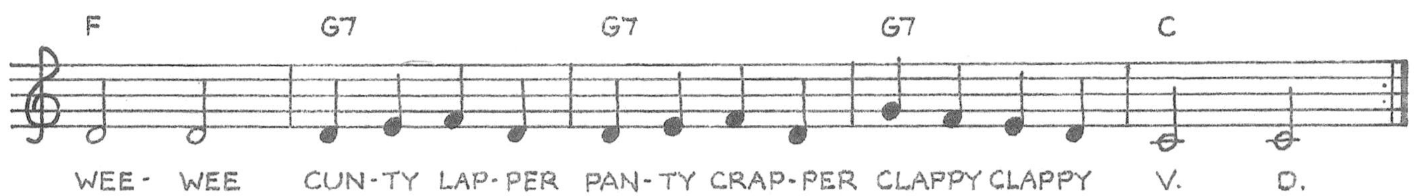
F G7 G7 G7 C
WEE- WEE CUN-TY LAP-PER PAN-TY CRAP-PER CLAPPY CLAPPY V. D.

2. PEEPEE CACA FUCKY-FUCK
CLITORAL VAGINEY
SUCKY HUMPY
STINKY DUMPY
STICK IT UP YOUR HEINEY

3. PEEPEE CACA FUCKY-FUCK
PEEPEE C.A.C.A.
POOPY POTTY
LICKY TWATTY
EXPLOSIVE DIARRHE-A

4. PEEPEE CACA FUCKY-FUCK
SPANKY CANKER SOREM
VERY HAIRY
DINGLEBERRY
FA LA LA SANTORUM

5. PEEPEE CACA FUCKY-FUCK
JACK IT OFF AND JIZZY
SHOW YOUR THINGY
CUNNILINGY
BUSY BUSY BUSY

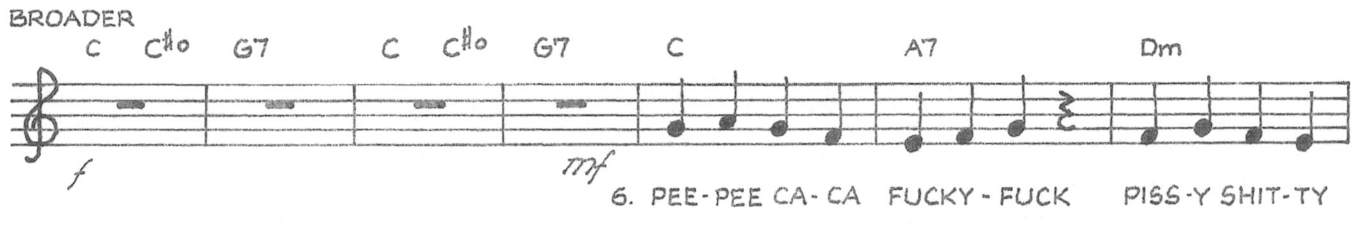
BROADER
C C♯o G7 C C♯o G7 C A7 Dm
f
mf
6. PEE-PEE CA-CA FUCKY-FUCK PISS-Y SHIT-TY

G7 Dm7 Fm6 G7 C
WEE- WEE CUN-TY LAP-PER PAN-TY CRAP-PER CLAPPY CLAPPY V. D.
rall.

WRITTEN FOR A "FILTHY SONG NIGHT"
AT THE JALOPY THEATER IN BROOKLYN

DECEMBER 2012

PEOPLE LIKE YOU

BRISK
Dm7 Dm7 Gm7 Gm7 C7
mf
VERSE
F F7 B♭
mf
PEOPLE LIKE YOU AND PEOPLE LIKE ME CANNOT GET ALONG, WE
B♭m F F7
BOTH A- GREE. SO WHAT WE SHOULD DO WITH PEOPLE LIKE YOU IS
B♭ C7 F
LOCK YOU IN A CELL AND THROW A- WAY THE KEY, THE
F7aug B♭ F
f
KEY. YOU CAN SIT THERE IN THE DARK,
C7 A7 B♭
PLAYING WITH THE RATS AND ROACH - ES. I'LL GO STROLL A-
F G7 C7
ROUND THE PARK, DE- LIVERED FROM YOUR RE- PROACH - ES: YOUR
C7 C7 C7
YAKETY YAKETY YAKETY YAKETY YAK, YOU ASS- HOLE.
SING VERSES 2 & 3

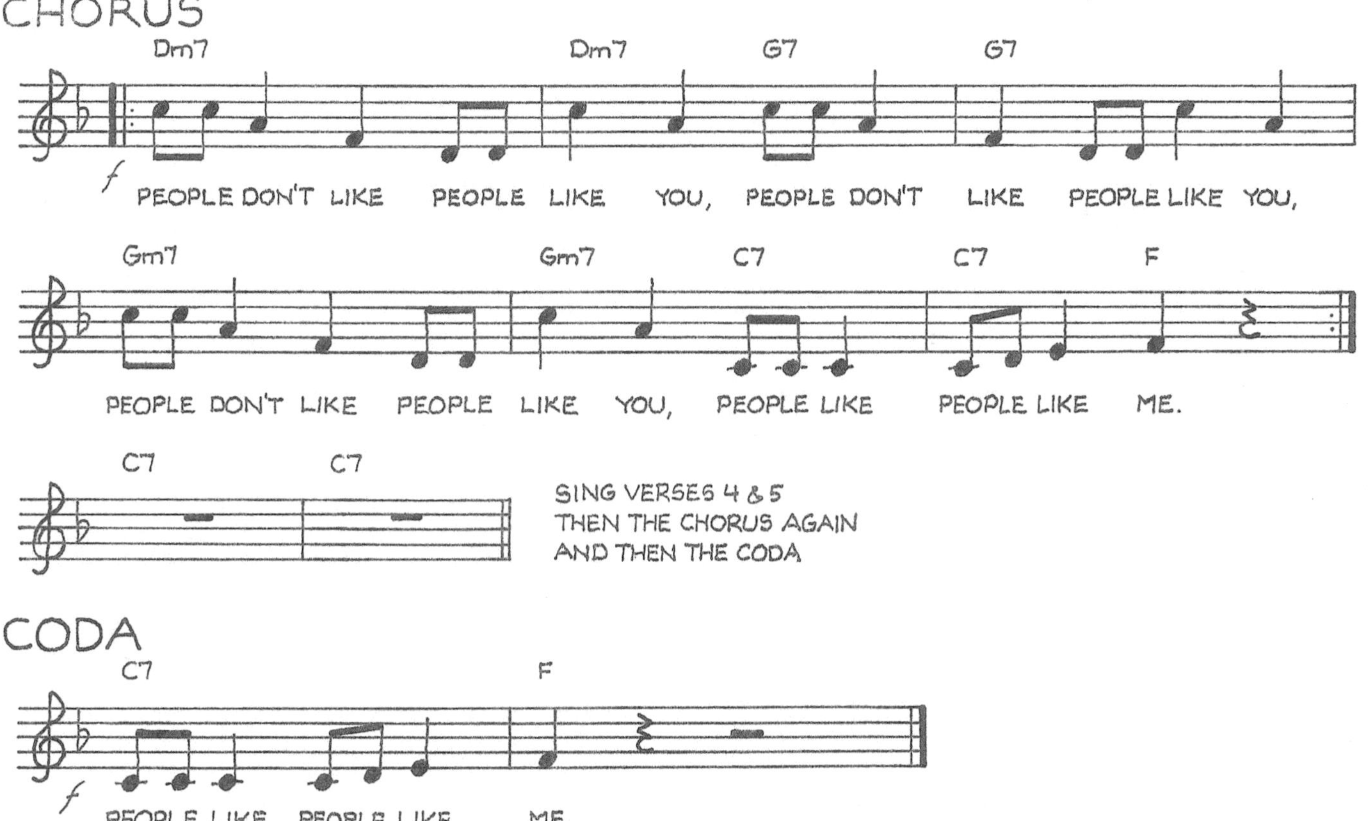
CHORUS
Dm7
Dm7
G7
G7
f
PEOPLE DON'T LIKE PEOPLE LIKE YOU, PEOPLE DON'T LIKE PEOPLE LIKE YOU,
Gm7
Gm7
C7
C7
F
PEOPLE DON'T LIKE PEOPLE LIKE YOU, PEOPLE LIKE PEOPLE LIKE ME.
C7
C7
SING VERSES 4 & 5
THEN THE CHORUS AGAIN
AND THEN THE CODA
CODA
C7
F
f
PEOPLE LIKE PEOPLE LIKE ME.

2. PEOPLE LIKE YOU AND PEOPLE LIKE ME
CANNOT GET ALONG, WE BOTH AGREE.
SO WHAT WE SHOULD DO
WITH PEOPLE LIKE YOU
IS DUMP YOU ON AN ISLAND IN THE CARIBBEE,
IBBEE.
YOU CAN STROLL AROUND THE PLACE,
HAPPY IN YOUR OWN DOMINION.
I WON'T HAVE TO SEE YOUR FACE
OR LISTEN TO YOUR OPINION:
YOUR YAKETY YAKETY YAKETY YAKETY YAK,
YOU ASSHOLE.

3. PEOPLE LIKE YOU AND PEOPLE LIKE ME
CANNOT GET ALONG, WE BOTH AGREE.
SO WHAT WE SHOULD DO
WITH PEOPLE LIKE YOU
IS PUT YOU ON A LEASH AND TIE YOU TO A TREE,
A TREE.
YOU CAN SIT THERE IN THE SHADE
WITH A COUPLE FEET OF FREEDOM.
I WON'T MISS THE POINTS YOU MADE.
I'VE NEVER BEEN KNOWN TO NEED 'EM:
YOUR YAKETY YAKETY YAKETY YAKETY YAK,
YOU ASSHOLE.

4. PEOPLE LIKE YOU AND PEOPLE LIKE ME
CANNOT GET ALONG, WE BOTH AGREE.
SO WHAT WE SHOULD DO
WITH PEOPLE LIKE YOU
IS PUT YOU ON A BOAT UPON A RAGING SEA,
A SEA.
YOU CAN RIDE UPON THE FOAM,
LEANING ON THE RAIL AND RETCHING.
MEANWHILE I'LL BE SAFE AT HOME
AVOIDING YOUR ENDLESS KVETCHING:
YOUR YAKETY YAKETY YAKETY YAKETY YAK,
YOU ASSHOLE.

5. PEOPLE LIKE YOU AND PEOPLE LIKE ME
CANNOT GET ALONG, WE BOTH AGREE.
SO WHAT WE SHOULD DO
WITH PEOPLE LIKE YOU
IS DUMP YOU IN A BARREL THAT IS FILLED WITH GHEE,
WITH GHEE,
YOU CAN WALLOW IN THE GREASE,
GETTING MORE MOROSE AND FATTER.
THAT WAY I'LL GET SOME RELEASE
FROM ALL OF YOUR STUPID CHATTER:
YOUR YAKETY YAKETY YAKETY YAKETY YAK,
YOU ASSHOLE.

JUNE 2013 · N.Y.C.

Ptooey

LANGUID AND REFLECTIVE
Gmaj7 G7 Cmaj7 Cm D7
mp
Gmaj7 C D7 G7
mp
AS YOU LIE, SOME CLOUDLESS NIGHT, GAZ- ING UP- WARDS AT THE SIGHT
Cmaj7 Cm G D7
OF THE STAR- RY SPANGLED CHA- OS LOOM- ING O- VER- HEAD,
Gmaj7 C Cm G
DO YOU SIM- PER, STRUCK WITH AWE? NO YOU DON'T, YOU STROKE YOUR JAW,
C C♯dim7 Cm D7
AND YOU SAD- LY MUR- MUR IN- STEAD: P-
Gmaj7 G7 Cmaj7 F7
TOO- EY, P- TOO- EY, IT'S ALL A LOT OF HOO- EY, A
Bm C7 E♭7 D7
PLATE OF AS- TRO- NOM- I- CAL CHOP SU- EY. FOO- EY. THE
Fmaj7 Em7 Cm G
U- NI- VERSE IS VER- Y BIG; YOU'RE AT A LOSS TO E- VEN FIG- URE

Cm F7 Gmaj7 G#dim7 Am7
OUT HOW BIG IT IS, IT'S SO IM- MENSE. IT'S FULL OF COM- ETS,
D7 G Am Bm7 C B7
STARS, AND PLAN- ETS; IT'S BEEN HERE SINCE TIME BE- GAN; IT'S VER- Y BIG AND
E7 A9 A9 G Cm
OLD AND MAKES NO SENSE. AND YOU DON'T CARE, AND I DON'T CARE: WE
Am7 D7 Gmaj7 G7
VIEW THE WHOLE THING WITH DE- SPAIR. P- TOO- EY, P- TOO- EY, IT'S
Cmaj7 F7 Bm C7
ALL MIXED UP AND SCREW- Y. AND WE DON'T CARE IF IT ALL GOES KA-
Eb7 D7 Gmaj7 Gmaj7
BLOO- EY, DO WE? P- TOO- EY.

MARCH 2016
NEW PALTZ, N.Y.

THE RENAISSANCE FAIRE

JAUNTY
Dm Dm Dm Dm Dm C Dm A
f
mp
BIL- LY, BIL-LY, YOU'VE BEEN BAD,
Dm C Dm A F C F C
YOU'RE IN DUTCH WITH MOM AND DAD. IF YOU'RE NOT BETTER YOU'D BETTER BEWARE, SOME
B♭ B♭ Am A
HOT SUMMER DAY THEY'LL TAKE YOU AWAY TO THE
Dm Gm Dm A
mf
RENAISSANCE FAIRE. THE
Dm Am Dm Am Gm C Gm A
RENAISSANCE FAIRE, THE RENAISSANCE FAIRE, THE LORDS AND THE LADIES HAVE LOOSENED THEIR HAIR. THEY'RE
RENAISSANCE FAIRE, THE RENAISSANCE FAIRE, COME SAMPLE THE MUTTON, THERE'S PLENTY TO SPARE. AND
C B♭ C B♭ A D
DANCING A JIG IN THEIR LONG UNDERWEAR HERE AT THE RENAISSANCE FAIRE.
QUAFF A FEW TANKARDS OF MEAD IF YOU DARE HERE AT THE RENAISSANCE FAIRE.
F C F C F C F C
WHERE OH WHERE IS THE COUNTESS OF KENT? SHE'S SOAKING HER FEET IN THE BACK OF THE TENT. SHE'S
WHERE OH WHERE IS THE GOOD FRIAR TUCK? HE'S WASHING HIS FROCK IN THE BACK OF THE TRUCK. HE

Dm C Dm B♭ C A
1.
GETTING A BLISTER BUT EARNING HER RENT. HEY DERRY DOWN HEY! THE
FELL IN THE FEAST WHEN HIS SANDAL GOT STUCK. HEY DERRY DOWN
2. ⟶
A B♭ C D B♭ Gm F Am
HEY! HEY DERRY DOWN HEY! JOUST- ING, JOUST- ING, WHICH
CHAIN MAIL, CHAIN MAIL, HE
Gm C F B♭ Gm F Am
GALLANT WILL WIN THE FAIR MAID? JOUST- ING, JOUST- ING, THEY
WORKED ON THAT SUIT FOR A YEAR. CHAIN MAIL, CHAIN MAIL, HE'S
Dm C Dm Gm C Dm
WISH THEY WERE BACK IN THE SHADE, BILLY, YOU WOULDN'T BELIEVE WHAT THEY'RE PAID, BILLY, YOU
AW-FULLY GLAD TO BE HERE, BILLY, LET'S HOPE THAT HE DOESN'T COME NEAR, BILLY, LET'S
Gm C Dm Gm C D
WOULDN'T BELIEVE WHAT THEY'RE PAID. THE
PRAY THAT HE DOESN'T COME NEAR.
Dm Am Dm Am Gm C Gm A
RENAISSANCE FAIRE, THE RENAISSANCE FAIRE, THE PIP-ERS ARE PLAYING A ROLLICKING AIR. WHAT
C C B♭ A D
WOULDN'T YOU GIVE FOR A COMFORTABLE CHAIR, HERE AT THE RENAISSANCE FAIRE.

F C F C F C F C
WHERE OH WHERE IS THE PUPPET SHOW MAN? HE'S DRINKING HIS GATORADE BACK IN THE VAN. HE
Dm C Dm B♭ C A
LOOKS LIKE HE'LL GET A RE- MARK-A-BLE TAN. HEY DERRY DOWN HEY!
Dm Dm Dm Dm Dm Dm A
f
mp
BIL- LY, BIL- LY, DON'T BE BAD,
Dm C Dm A F C F C
DON'T MAKE DAD AND MOM- MY MAD. IF YOU ACT SULKY AND SAY YOU DON'T CARE, SOME
B♭ B♭ Am A
DAY YOU MAY FIND THEY'VE LEFT YOU BEHIND AT THE
Dm Gm Dm A D
RENAISSANCE FAIRE.

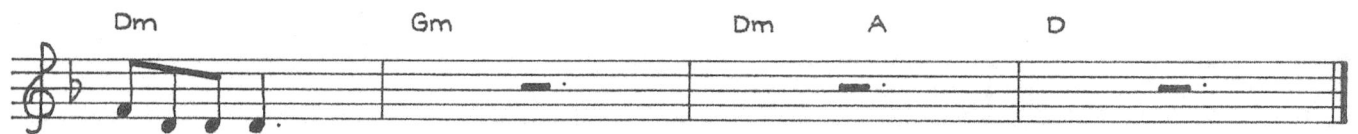

JUNE 1998 - N.Y.C.

THE ROSE

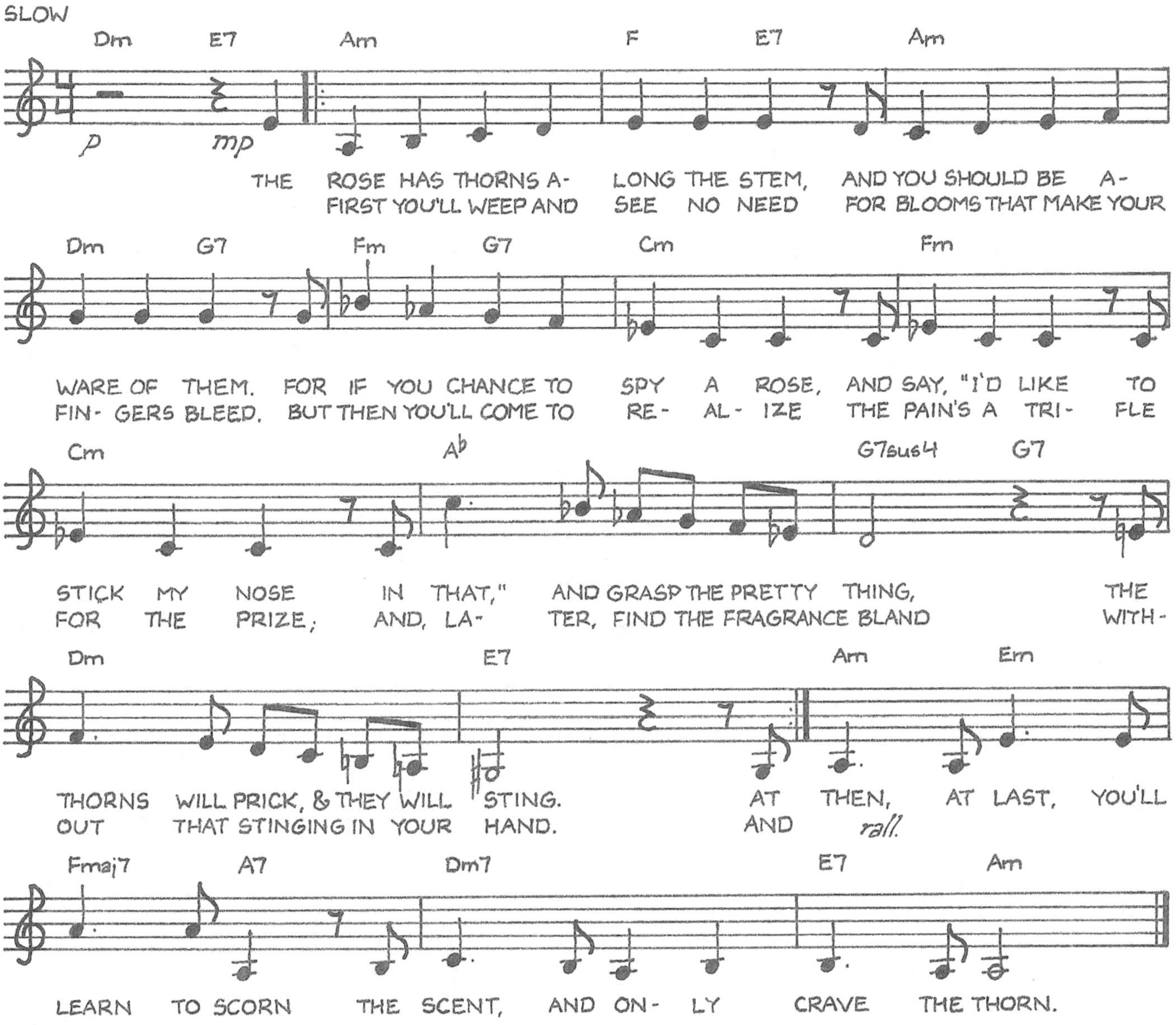

SLOW

Dm E7 Am F E7 Am

p *mp*

THE ROSE HAS THORNS A- LONG THE STEM, AND YOU SHOULD BE A-
FIRST YOU'LL WEEP AND SEE NO NEED FOR BLOOMS THAT MAKE YOUR

Dm G7 Fm G7 Cm Fm

WARE OF THEM. FOR IF YOU CHANCE TO SPY A ROSE, AND SAY, "I'D LIKE TO
FIN- GERS BLEED. BUT THEN YOU'LL COME TO RE- AL- IZE THE PAIN'S A TRI- FLE

Cm A♭ G7sus4 G7

STICK MY NOSE IN THAT," AND GRASP THE PRETTY THING, THE
FOR THE PRIZE; AND, LA- TER, FIND THE FRAGRANCE BLAND WITH-

Dm E7 Am Em

THORNS WILL PRICK, & THEY WILL STING. AT THEN, AT LAST, YOU'LL
OUT THAT STINGING IN YOUR HAND. AND *rall.*

Fmaj7 A7 Dm7 E7 Am

LEARN TO SCORN THE SCENT, AND ON- LY CRAVE THE THORN.

SEPTEMBER 2012 - N.Y.C.

SOMEBODY SAID SOMETHING OFFENSIVE

A STEADY MODERATO
A♭7 C6 A♭7 C6 F
mp
A♭7 C6 A♭7
mf SOMEBODY SAID SOME- THING OF- FEN- SIVE. SOMEBODY SAID SOME- THING THAT
G7 G7 B♭7
MADE ME FEEL UN- COMF- T'RA- BLE. SOMEBODY SAID SOME- THING OF-
D6 F7 E♭maj7 C7 C7
FEN- SIVE. HOW COULD THEY DO THIS TO ME?
Fm7 B♭7 Gm C7
I WAS A- SLEEP IN MY CHAIR. NOW I'M COM- PLETE-LY AD-
D7 Gm7 C7
RENALIZED. THAT DOESN'T STRIKE ME AS FAIR.
Gm A7 Dm C7 F
WHY CAN'T THEY BE PENALIZED? SOMEONE SHOULD PAY FOR THIS
A♭7 C6 A♭7
SOMEBODY SAID SOME- THING OF- FEN- SIVE. SOMEBODY SAID SOME- THING COM-

G7
G7
B♭7
PLETE- LY IN- AP- PRO- PRI- ATE. SOMEBODY SAID SOME- THING OF-
D6
Gm7
C7
A7
Dm
FEN- SIVE. NOW FREE-DOM OF SPEECH IS O- KAY I WOULD SAY — I'LL DE-
G7
Gm7
C7
F
E7
FEND THE FIRST AMENDMENT TILL MY DY- ING DAY. BUT I OUGHT TO HAVE THE RIGHT TO MAKE IT
Am7
D7
A♭7
C6
JUST GO A- WAY WHEN SOMEBODY SAYS SOME- THING OF- FEN- SIVE.
A♭7
G7
G7
SOMEBODY SAYS SOME- THING THAT I DON'T WANT TO HEAR A- BOUT. WHEN
B♭7
D6
B♭7
SOMEBODY MAKES ME FEEL DE- FEN- SIVE, SOMEBODY MAKES ME AP- PRE-
D6
B♭7
D6
HEN- SIVE, SOMEBODY MAKES ME HY- PER- TEN- SIVE.
E♭
D7
G7
C6
C6
WHY MUST THE LAW BE SO COM- PRE- HENSIVE?

DECEMBER 1991 - N.Y.C.
REVISED MARCH 2016
NEW PALTZ, N.Y.

SON OF A GUN

SOMEWHAT BRISK
C C C G7 C
mp mf
1. FRED HAD A GUN. HE LIKED THE GUN A LOT: THE
G7 C D7 G7 Am
GUN WAS LOTS OF FUN; THE GUN WAS OFTEN SHOT. FRED HAD A SON, A
Dm E7 Dm E7 D7
SON A LOT LIKE FRED. AND WHEN HE FOUND THE GUN, HE BLEW OFF HALF HIS
G7 C D7
HEAD. SON OF A GUN, A GUN WILL KILL. SON OF A
G7 C F
GUN, AND OFTEN WILL. FRED HAD A SON, AND
1&2
C G7 C
NOW HE HAS NONE. SON OF A GUN.
3
G7 3 C
YOU YOU SON OF A BITCH.

2. FRED HAD A WIFE,
AND SHE WAS SO DISTRAUGHT
HER SON HAD LOST HIS LIFE
THAT SHE AND FREDDY FOUGHT.
WHEN THEY WERE DONE,
THE WIFE LAY ON THE FLOOR;
FOR FREDDY HAD A GUN,
AND THAT'S WHAT GUNS ARE FOR.
SON OF A GUN,
A GUN CAN KILL.
SON OF A GUN,
AND OFTEN WILL.
NOW, THANKS TO FRED,
BOTH SON AND WIFE ARE DEAD,
SON OF A GUN.

3. FRED IN DISMAY
STOOD WITH HIS GUN IN HAND.
HE'D HAD AN AWFUL DAY;
IT HADN'T GONE AS PLANNED.
FRED, WHILE YOU'RE HERE,
WRAP UP YOUR SHOOTING SPREE.
JUST AIM IT AT YOUR EAR,
AND MAKE THOSE CORPSES THREE.
SON OF A GUN,
A GUN CAN KILL.
SON OF A GUN,
AND OFTEN WILL.
FRED, FOLLOW THROUGH,
SO WE'LL BE RID OF YOU,
YOU SON OF A BITCH.

AUGUST 2014
N.Y.C.

Uncle's Ankles

LIVELY
C C C
mp mf
1. UNCLE BERTIE LIKED TO LOOK THROUGH
C C G D7 G
TRASH. HE LIKED TO LOOK FOR THINGS THAT HE COULD TURN TO CASH. BUT
F C E7 Am D7
SINCE THE TRASH IS DIRTY, IT IN- FECTED UNCLE BERTIE, AND HE DEVELOPED QUITE A PAINFUL
G7 F E7
RASH. THERE'S A RASH ON UNCLE'S AN- KLES. HOW IT
Dm G7 Am Dm G7
HURTS, AND HOW IT RAN- KLES. HE SET OUT TO MAKE SOME MONEY, NOW THE
C A7 F G7 C
SORES ARE RAW AND RUNNY ON THE RASH ON UNCLE'S AN- KLES.

2. UNCLE BERTIE WADED IN THE STREAM,
WHEN SUDDENLY HE LET OUT QUITE A
PIERCING SCREAM.
A PASSING GROUP OF LEECHES
FOUND THEIR WAY INTO HIS BREECHES,
AND LEFT HIM MANY MARKS OF THEIR ESTEEM.
THERE ARE BITES ON UNCLE'S ANKLES;
HOW IT HURTS, AND HOW IT RANKLES.
HE WENT WADING IN THE WATER,
NOW THE DOCTOR HAS TO CAUTER-
IZE THE BITES
ON UNCLE'S ANKLES.

3. BERTIE WENT OUT STROLLING IN THE ZOO.
HE SMILED UPON A LADY WITH A
HOW ARE YOU.
THE LADY WASN'T FLIRTY,
AND EXPRESSED TO UNCLE BERTIE
DISPLEASURE AT HIS ACTIONS WITH HER SHOE.
THERE'S A BRUISE ON UNCLE'S ANKLES;
HOW IT HURTS, AND HOW IT RANKLES.
NOW THE DAMAGE FROM HER SNEAKER
MAKES HIS WALK A LITTLE WEAKER,
WITH THAT BRUISE
ON UNCLE'S ANKLES.

4. UNCLE BERTIE WOKE UP FROM HIS NAP,
AND HEADED FOR THE OUTHOUSE FOR A
NICE LONG CRAP.
BUT THEN HE STUCK HIS LOAFER
IN A HOLE LEFT BY A GOPHER,
AND FELL UPON HIS BELLY WITH A SNAP.
THERE'S A BREAK IN UNCLE'S ANKLES;
HOW IT HURTS, AND HOW IT RANKLES.
NOW HE GETS AROUND ON CRUTCHES,
AND IT HURTS HIM WHEN HE TOUCHES
WHERE IT BROKE
ON UNCLE'S ANKLES.

5. BERTIE THOUGHT HE'D TAKE A WALK AROUND.
HE TRIPPED AND TOOK A TUMBLE ON THE
GRASSY GROUND.
IT'S PAINFUL WHEN YOU SETTLE
IN A BED OF STINGING NETTLE
THAT'S LIKE THE ONE THAT UNCLE BERTIE FOUND.
THERE ARE STINGS IN UNCLE'S ANKLES;
HOW IT HURTS, AND HOW IT RANKLES.
NOW HE WHIMPERS AND HE WHEEDLES
FOR RELIEF FROM ALL THE NEEDLES
THAT ARE STUCK
IN UNCLE'S ANKLES.

6. BERTIE TRIED TO WALK ACROSS THE COALS.
HE BRAVED THE SMOKING CINDERS WITH HIS
TWO BARE SOLES.
DESPITE INTENSIVE TRAINING,
MEDITATION AND EXPLAINING,
NOW BERTIE'S FEET ARE FULL OF LITTLE HOLES.
THERE ARE BURNS ON UNCLE'S ANKLES;
HOW IT HURTS, AND HOW IT RANKLES.
BERTIE'S WALK WAS QUITE A SCORCHER,
NOW THE AFTERMATH IS TORTURE
WITH THOSE BURNS
ON UNCLE'S ANKLES.

7. THEN ONE MORNING BERTIE TOOK THE AIR
AND MET A VERY HUNGRY AND E-
NORMOUS BEAR,
WHICH ATE UP UNCLE BERTIE
SO COMPLETELY THAT IN THIRTY
MINUTES THERE WAS VERY LITTLE THERE.
ALL THAT'S LEFT IS UNCLE'S ANKLES;
HOW IT HURTS, AND HOW IT RANKLES.
THEY WERE MAGNETS FOR DISASTER,
BUT THEY DID OUTLAST THEIR MASTER.
ALL THAT'S LEFT
IS UNCLE'S ANKLES.

JULY 2014
N.Y.C.

Viola

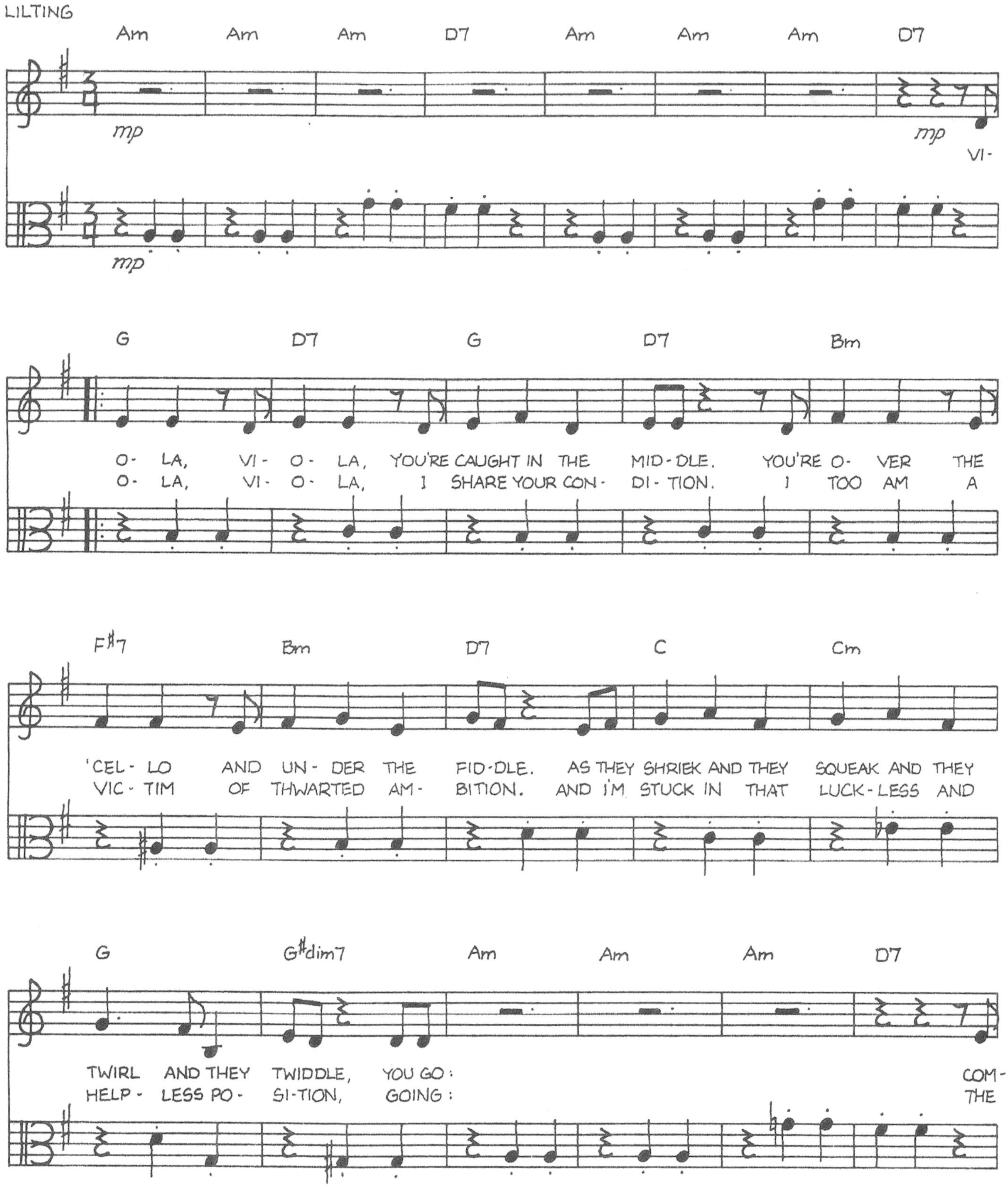

LILTING

Am Am Am D7 Am Am Am D7

mp *mp*

VI-

mp

G D7 G D7 Bm

O- LA, VI- O- LA, YOU'RE CAUGHT IN THE MID-DLE. YOU'RE O- VER THE
O- LA, VI- O- LA, I SHARE YOUR CON- DI- TION. I TOO AM A

F♯7 Bm D7 C Cm

'CEL- LO AND UN- DER THE FID-DLE. AS THEY SHRIEK AND THEY SQUEAK AND THEY
VIC- TIM OF THWARTED AM- BITION. AND I'M STUCK IN THAT LUCK-LESS AND

G G♯dim7 Am Am Am D7

TWIRL AND THEY TWIDDLE, YOU GO: COM-
HELP- LESS PO- SI-TION, GOING: THE

F#m
C#7
F#m
G7
Bm
PO - SERS ARE LA - ZY AND FOOL - ISH AND MEAN; THEY JUST WRITE YOU
WORLD HAS RE - FUSED US AT - TEN - TION AND LOVE. WE'RE SNUBBED FROM BE -

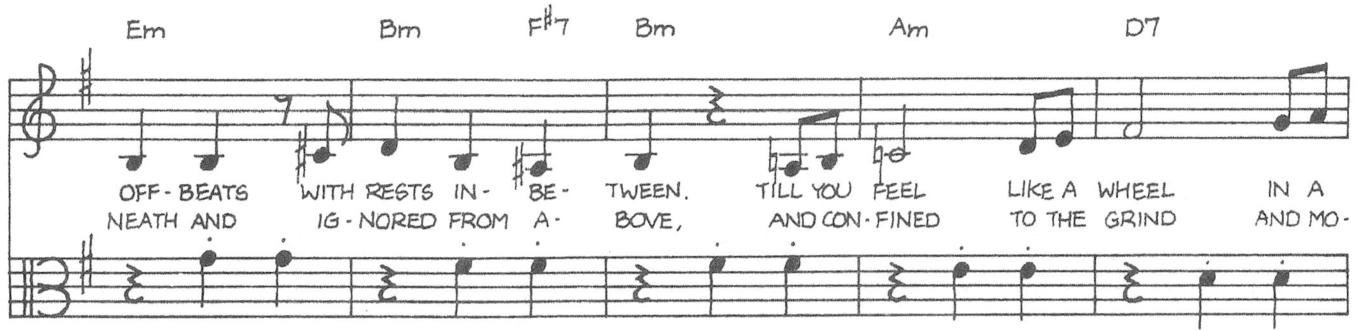
Em
Bm
F#7
Bm
Am
D7
OFF - BEATS WITH RESTS IN - BE - TWEEN. TILL YOU FEEL LIKE A WHEEL IN A
NEATH AND IG - NORED FROM A - BOVE, AND CON - FINED TO THE GRIND AND MO -

Gm
Cm
Am
Am
Am
D7
mf
FIEND - ISH MA - CHINE, GOING: VI -
NOT - O - NY OF GOING: VI -

G
E7
Am
D7aug
G
O - LA, VI - O - LA, YOU'VE STO - LEN MY HEART, FOR YOUR EX - QUIS - ITE
O - LA, VI - O - LA, YOU'VE SET ME A FLAME. YOU'RE AS SWEET AS THE
mf

Em
C
B7
Em
C
AL - TO'S THE ES - SENCE OF ART, AND I PRAY FOR THE DAY WHEN YOUR
FLOW - ER THAT GAVE YOU YOUR NAME, AND I WEEP THAT YOU KEEP ON EN -

C#dim7
D7
Am
Am
Am
SO - LO WILL START, AND THE END OF THAT OOM - PA - PA OOM - PA - PA
DUR - ING THE SHAME OF THAT OOM - PA - PA OOM - PA - PA AL - WAYS THE

1.
D7
Am
Am
Am
D7
PART. VI -
SAME.

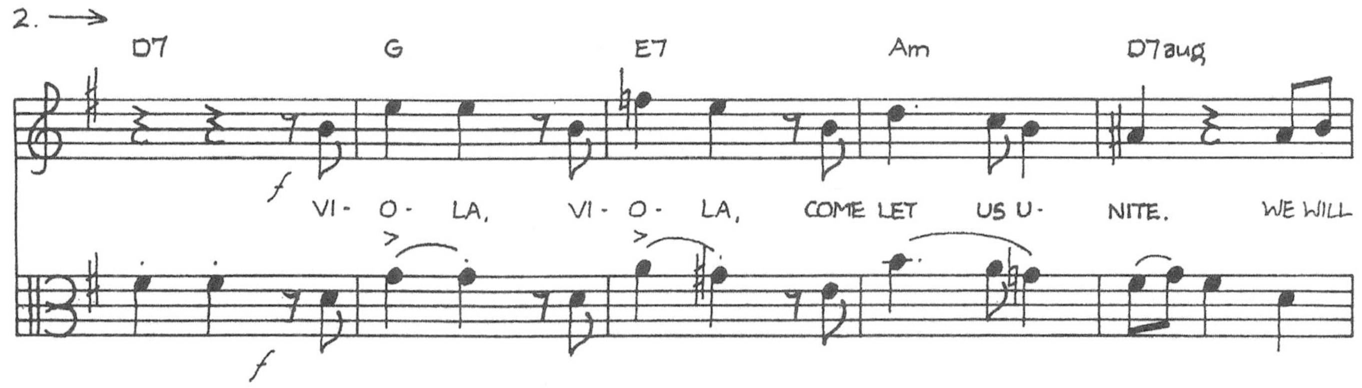
2.
D7
G
E7
Am
D7aug
f
VI - O - LA, VI - O - LA, COME LET US U - NITE. WE WILL
f

G Em C B7 Em
MARCH ON TO- GETH- ER AND FIGHT THE GOOD FIGHT, TILL WE GAZE ON THAT
C C#dim7 D7 Am Am
BLAZ- ING AND GLOR- I- OUS SIGHT OF THE DAWN AT THE END OF THE
Am D7 Am Am D7 G
OOM- PA- PA NIGHT. OF THE DAWN AT THE END OF THE OOM- PA- PA NIGHT.

OCTOBER 1998 - N.Y.C.

WE ALL WORK SO HARD

(WHEN NONE OF US WANT TO WORK AT ALL)

LAZY
F Fdim7 Gm7 C7 F Fdim7 Gm7 C7
mp
mp
I'M
F Fdim7 Gm7 C7 F Fdim7
TOLD THAT WORK ENNOBLES MAN AND LIFTS HIS SPIRIT HIGH, THAT HAP- PI- NESS IS ON- LY HAD IN
Gm7 C7 F D♭7 Gm7 C7
DRUDGING TILL WE DIE. BUT I DON'T SEE WHY. I'M
F Fdim7 Gm7 C7 F Fdim7
TOLD THAT MAN IS MORE DIVINE WHEN SHACKLED TO A PLOW, THAT BREAD IS SOMEHOW SWEETER WHEN IT'S
Gm7 C7 F D♭7 Gm7 C7
SOAKED IN SWEAT OF BROW. BUT I DON'T SEE HOW. DOES
Am D7 B♭maj7
PASTING LA- BELS ON-TO JARS OR WAITRESSING IN COCKTAIL BARS PROMOTE THE DIG- NI- TY OF MAN IN
G7 Gm7 C7
SOME BIZARRE CELESTIAL PLAN? I DON'T SEE HOW IT CAN. IF
F Fdim7 Gm7 C7 F Fdim7
WE WERE FREE TO FOLLOW ALL THE DICTATES OF THE SOUL, WE EACH WOULD OPT FOR UNEMPLOYMENT

Gm7 A7 Dm G7
EASE AND IN-DO-LENT ENJOYMENT, HAVING NO GREATER GOAL THAN TO
B♭ B♭m F C7 C7
CONTEMPLATE OUR USELESSNESS BE-NEATH A EU-CA-LYP-TUS. BUT
B♭ B♭m F C7 C7
THAT IS NOT THE LIFE WITH WHICH SO-CI-E-TY'S EQUIPPED US. FOR
SLOWER
F E7 E♭7 D7 G7 Gdim7 G7 Gm7 C7
WE ALL WORK SO HARD, WHEN NONE OF US WANT TO WORK AT
F Fdim7 C7 Gm7 C7 Gm7 A7
ALL. WE'VE GOT TO GET UP AT EIGHT TO DO SOMETHING BORING, WHEN WE'D
Dm G7 B♭ F G7 Dm G7
RATHER SLEEP LATE, CON-TEN-TED-LY SNORING. SOMEWHERE, SOMETHING WENT A-
Gm7 C7 Am A7 Dm G7
MISS. LIFE IS DIS-MAL, IT'S ABYS-MAL, OFTEN CURSED BY DISAPPOINTMENT, BUT THE
Dm G7 Gm7 C7 F E7 E♭7 D7
WORST FLY IN THE OINTMENT IS THIS: THAT WE ALL WORK SO

G7 Gdim7 G7 Gm7 C7 Gm7 C7
HARD, WHEN I DON'T WANT TO WORK, AND YOU DON'T WANT TO WORK, AND
Gm7 C7 A7 Dm G7 Gm7 C7
NONE OF US WANT TO WORK AT ALL, AT ALL. NONE OF US WANT TO WORK AT
Dm G7 Gm7 C7 B♭m F
ALL, AT ALL. NONE OF US WANT TO WORK AT ALL.

MARCH 1987
SYDNEY/N.Y.C.

We Need More Art

A JAUNTY MARCH
Ddim7 D7 Ddim7 D7 Em C7
f
f
WE NEED MORE ART:
WE NEED MORE ART:
F♮ E7 Em C7
PAINT SOME SLOGANS ON A WHITEWASHED WALL. WE NEED MORE ART:
BANG A RHYTHM ON A GAR- BAGE CAN. WE NEED MORE ART:
F♮ E7 Am7 D7 F♯7 Bm
FILM YOUR BUDDIES IN THE LO- CAL MALL. DON'T HOLD BACK, JUST GO CRE- ATE IT,
SNAP A PHOTO OF A HOMELESS MAN. STIR UP YOUR CRE- A- TIVE JUIC- ES,
Am7 D7 F♯7 Bm C Bm E7
THEN BE SURE TO SIGN AND DATE IT. DON'T FEEL BAD IF PEO- PLE HATE IT:
CHURN IT OUT WITH- OUT EX- CUS- ES. MAK- ING SOME-THING WITH NO USE IS
A7 Am7 D7 A7 A7 Am7 D7
GOOD WORK IS CON- TRO- VER- SIAL.
ES- SEN- TIAL TO OUR CUL- TURE.
C C Bm E7 Am
mf
TELL THE WORLD YOUR JOYS AND GRIEFS. AIR YOUR PO-
Am Cm D7 C C
LIT- I- CAL BE- LIEFS. ADD YOUR EF- FORTS TO THE

Bm E7 Am B7 C
WORLD'S SUP- PLY. DON'T BE SHY. YOU CAN MAKE A
Em Am B♭ Am7 D7
LOT OF ART IF YOU ON- LY TRY.
Ddim7 D7 Am7 B♭9 E♭maj7
WE NEED MORE ART: FILL A BOTTLE WITH A
D7 Am7 B♭9 E♭maj7
THOUSAND ANTS. WE NEED MORE ART: DRAW THE PRESIDENT WITH-
D7 Edim7 E7 Edim7 E7 Edim7 E7 Edim7 E7
OUT HIS PANTS. PAINT A PORTRAIT, SCRAWL A SON-NET, BUILD A BOX WITH DIL-DOES ON IT,
D7 C Bm G G♯dim7 Am7 D7 Am7
KNIT A TI- NY EAST-ER BON-NET. GO OUT AND BE CRE-A- TIVE. WE NEED MORE
B♭9 E♭maj7 D7 Am7
ART: WRITE A MONOLOGUE A- BOUT YOUR MOM. WE NEED MORE
B♭9 E♭maj7 D7 E♮maj7
ART: PASTE YOUR PICTURE ON A C. D. ROM. DANCE A SOLO WITH A

E♭7
F♮maj7
E♮7
G♭maj7
BAS- KET- BALL, MAKE A MANNEQUIN THAT'S TEN FEET TALL, WRITE A SYMPHONY FOR
F♮7
G♮maj7
F♯7
A♭maj7
SOU- SA- PHONES, COAT A URINAL WITH ICE CREAM CONES, WEAVE A BASKET OUT OF
G7
A♮maj7
G♯7
Adim7 A7
HU- MAN HAIR, FOLD SOME O-RI-GA-MI UN- DER- WEAR, PEN A ONE - ACT,
Adim7 A7 Adim7 A7 Adim7 A7 Adim7 A7
DO SOME SKETCHING, CAST A PLAS- TER, ETCH AN ETCH- ING, SCULPT A SCULPTURE,
Adim7 A7 Adim7 A7 Adim7 A7 Em
DRAW A DOO- DLE, TAPE A SOUND PIECE, SHAVE A POO - DLE, ff WE NEED MORE ART,
Em E7 E7 G
WE NEED MORE ART, WE NEED MORE ART, WE NEED MORE ART, WE
Em A7 G♯dim7 G♮ A7 D D
NEED MORE ART! WE NEED IT NOW!

DECEMBER 1995
N.Y.C.

THE WORSE IT GETS, THE BETTER WE LIKE IT

FAST
THE WORSE IT GETS, THE BETTER WE LIKE IT.
WE LIKE IT BETTER THE WORSE IT GETS. WE TAKE NAPS AS THE WORLD COL- LAPS - ES,
WE KICK BACK AND COOL OUR JETS. THE WORSE IT GETS, THE BETTER WE LIKE IT,
WE LIKE IT BETTER THE WORSE IT GETS. WE JUST BINGE AS THE WORLD UN- HING - ES,
NO ONE FUSS - ES, NO ONE FRETS. FA LA LA LA LA LA LA.
HEY! WE DON'T CARE, WE'RE
MUCH TOO DEB - O - NAIR. THE WORLD MAY CRUM - BLE, BUT

D7
D7
G7
G7
WE WON'T GRUM - BLE, WE'LL JUST SIT BACK ON OUR COL-
D7
G7
Gdim7
G7
LEC- TIVE DER-RI- ERE. JUST BE- CAUSE IT'S THERE.
Gdim7
G7
G7
G7
JUST BE- CAUSE IT'S THERE.
D7
G7
C
C
HEY! THE WORSE IT GETS THE BETTER WE LIKE IT,
G7
G7
C
C
C
WE LIKE IT BETTER THE WORSE IT GETS. HEY! HEY!
C
C
A♭
A♭
HEY! HEY! HEY HEY! WE LIKE IT BETTER THE WORSE IT GETS, THE
E♭7
Fm
G7
G7
C
G7
C
WORSE IT GETS, THE BETTER WE LIKE IT, WE LIKE IT BETTER THE WORSE IT GETS, THE
D7
G7
C
D7
G7
WORSE IT GETS THE BETTER WE LIKE IT. DOO- BIE DOO- BIE DUM DUM DUM.

D7 G7 E7 E7
f HEY! mp WE DON'T MIND, WE'RE
Am E7 Am F F
NOT THE ANX- IOUS KIND. THE WORLD MAY SHAT- TER, BUT
D7 D7 G7 G7
mf THAT WON'T MAT- TER, WE'LL JUST SIT BACK ON OUR COL-
D7 G7 Gdim7 G7
LEC - TIVE BE- HIND. f IT'S NOT HARD TO FIND.
Gdim7 G7 G7 G7
f IT'S NOT HARD TO FIND.
D7 G7 C C
f HEY! mf THE WORSE IT GETS, THE BETTER WE LIKE IT,
G7 G7 C C
WE LIKE IT BETTER THE WORSE IT GETS. f NO REGRETS. NO UP- SETS.
C C D7 D7
mp LET'S GO DO SOME PIR- OU- ETTES, mf FOR THE WORSE IT GETS, THE BETTER WE

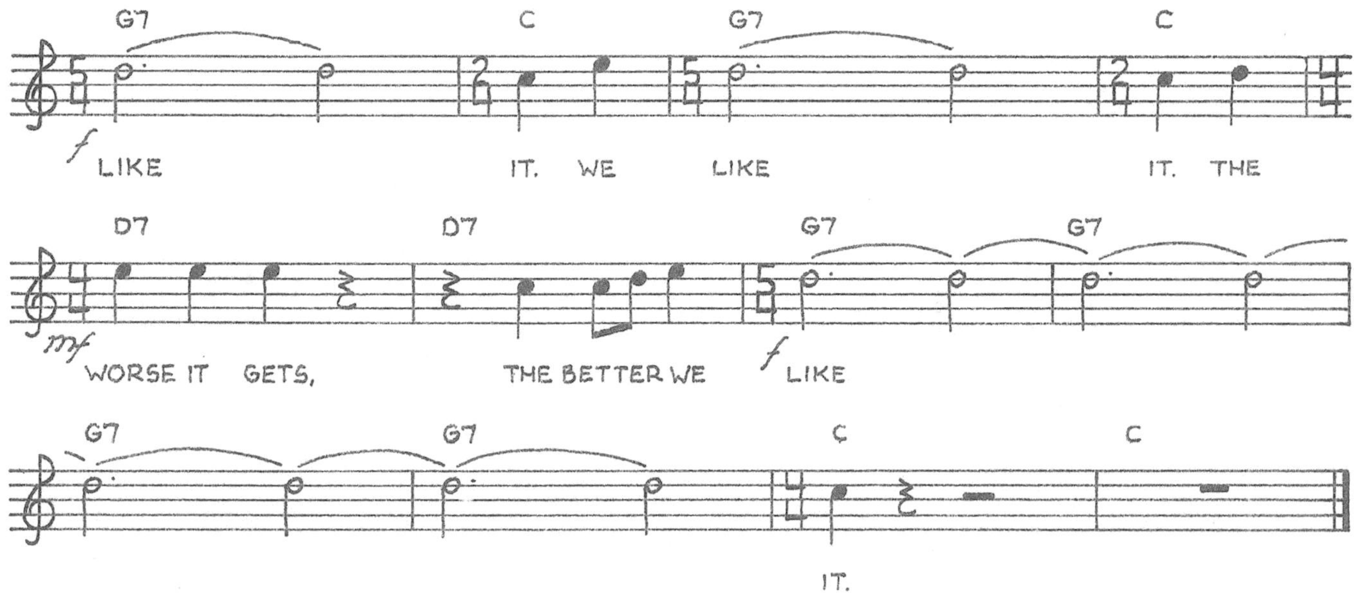
G7
C
G7
C
LIKE
IT. WE
LIKE
IT. THE
D7
D7
G7
G7
WORSE IT GETS,
THE BETTER WE
LIKE
G7
G7
C
C
IT.

MARCH 1990
N.Y.C.

Worthless Little Moments

RELAXED AND FLOWING
F
F Gm7 F F Gm7
mp
F F Gm7 F F Gm7
mp
TIME JUST SLIPS AWAY, TIME JUST DRIPS AWAY,
F G7 Gm7 Am Fdim7
STUMBLING A- STRAY, DAY AFTER DAY,
p
WHERE DOES IT GO?
Fdim7 Gm7 C7 Gm7 C7 Gm7 C7
I THINK THAT I KNOW.
mp
IN
Gm7 A7 Dm7
WORTH- LESS LIT- TLE MO- MENTS THAT ARE DEAD IN THE WA-
Dm7 G7 C7
TER. WHEN YOU SORT OF DOZE, IN AN I- DLE POSE, WITH YOUR
F D7 Gm7
FIN- GER HALF- WAY UP YOUR NOSE,
mf
IN VA- CANT LIT- TLE
A7 Dm7 G7
MO- MENTS WHEN YOUR BRAIN IS ON THE BLINK. WHEN YOU

Gm7
C7
F7
SORT OF SHRINK, WHILE THE THOUGHTS YOU THINK RE- FUSE SOME- HOW TO
F7
B♭
B♮dim7
Am
INTERLINK. YOU'RE SOME-WHAT OF A WRITE-OFF WITH YOUR IN- TER- NAL
Dm
G7
G7
Gm7
p
LIGHT OFF. BUT AS YOU KEEP UN- RAVELING, TIME JUST KEEPS ON
C7
F
Gdim7
mf
TRAV-EL-ING. I KNOW THAT WHEN A MAN DIES, HE'LL VIS- U- AL- IZE HIS
Dm7
G7
Am
LIFE PA-RAD- ING BE- FORE HIS EYES, SO IT SHOULD COME AS
B♭
A7
Gm7
A7
Gm7
NO SUR-PRISE TO ME TO SEE JUST WAST- ED LIT- TLE
A7
Dm7
G7
mp
MO- MENTS WHEN MY GEARS WERE DIS-EN- GAGED. JUST
Gm7
C7
Fdim7
p
WORTH- LESS LIT- TLE MO- MENTS THAT ARE DEAD IN THE WA-

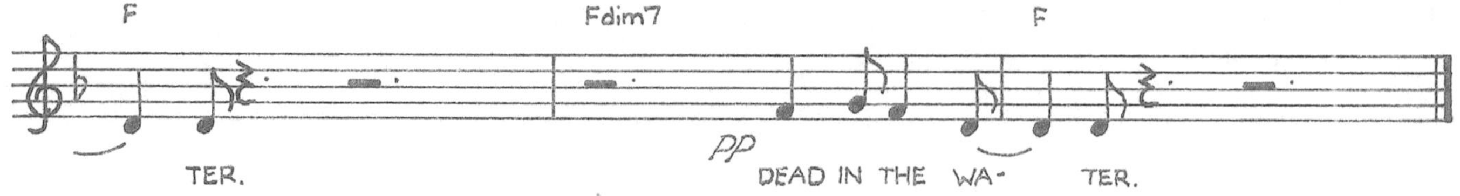
F
Fdim7
F
TER.
pp
DEAD IN THE WA- TER.

FEBRUARY 1990
N.Y.C.

Your Parents

FREELY
C G7 C Em7
mp mp
YOUR FA- THER DID- N'T WANT A KID: THAT'S
F Fm C Em7 A7
WHY HE DRANK THE WAY HE DID. YOUR MOTH-ER DROPPED A BRIGHT CA-REER TO
Dm G7 C Em7
COP- U- LATE AND BRING YOU HERE. THEY SCRAPPED THEIR DREAMS AND SCOTCHED THEIR JOYS TO
F Fm C Em7 A7
KEEP YOU STOCKED WITH FOOD AND TOYS, AND EVE- RY DAY THEY LIVED, RE- VILED THE
Dm G7 C Em7
ACT THAT SAD- DLED THEM WITH CHILD. BUT THOUGH THEY MADE YOUR LIFE A HELL, AND
F E7 Am G7 F Fm
mf
LEFT YOU ANX- IOUS AND UN- WELL, AND IN SUCH PAIN YOU BANG YOUR HEAD A-
C D7 Dm G7
mp
GAINST YOUR WALL, BE COM- FORT- ED. THEY MIXED ONE PEARL WITH THEIR A- BUSE: THEY
C F Fm C
TAUGHT YOU NOT TO RE- PRO- DUCE.
JUNE 2012 - N.Y.C.

ABOUT DOUG SKINNER

Doug Skinner has contributed articles and cartoons to *Black Scat Review, Oulipo Pornobongo, The Fortean Times, Strange Attractor Journal, Fate, Weirdo, The Anomalist, Nickelodeon, Cabinet,* and other fine publications. Black Scat has published several books of his stories and cartoons, as well as his translations of the French humorist Alphonse Allais.

He has written music for several dance companies, including ODC-San Francisco and Margaret Jenkins; his scores for actor/clown Bill Irwin include *The Regard of Flight*, *The Courtroom*, *The Regard Evening*, and *The Harlequin Studies*. He has performed his songs (the ones inside this book) in many theaters, clubs, and cabarets. His puppet shows with Michael Smith have been seen everywhere from Caroline's Comedy Club in Manhattan to the Museum of Contemporary Art in Los Angeles.

TV and movie appearances include *Great Performances*, *The '90s*, *Martin Mull's Talent Takes a Holiday*, *Ed*, *Crocodile Dundee II*, and a smattering of commercials.

He lived for decades in Manhattan, but has moved to New Paltz, a few miles to the north.

Selected
BLACK SCAT BOOKS

I AM SARCEY
Alphonse Allais

THE DETECTIVE WHO DIDN'T HAVE A CLUE
Alain Arias-Misson

DANTE'S FOIL & OTHER SPORTING TALES
Mark Axelrod

SISTER CARRIE CAME
Tom Bussmann

SWEET AND VICIOUS
Suzanne Burns

THREE PLAYS BY D. HARLAN WILSON

THE ZOMBIE OF GREAT PERU
Pierre-Corneille Blessebois

WHEN I GROW UP & OTHER MANTRAS
Terri Lloyd

CROCODILE SMILES: SHORT SHRIFT FICTIONS
Yuriy Tarnawsky

HERE LIES MEMORY: A PITTSBURGH NOVEL
Doug Rice

OULIPO PORNOBONGO
Various

CURIOUS IMPOSSIBILTIES
Carla M. Wilson

SLEEPYTIME CEMETERY: 40 STORIES
Doug Skinner

SACRED SINS
John Diamond-Nigh

VAHAZAR
Stanisław Ignacy Witkiewicz

www.ingramcontent.com/pod-product-compliance
Lightning Source LLC
LaVergne TN
LVHW081317060426
835509LV00015B/1569
* 9 7 8 0 9 9 9 2 6 2 2 2 1 *